WIRED
for
SUCCESS

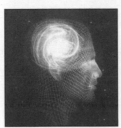

PROGRAMMED
for
FAILURE

WIRED *for* SUCCESS

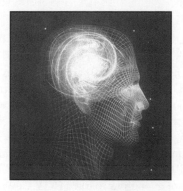

PROGRAMMED *for* FAILURE

DR. JAMES B. RICHARDS

NATIONAL BEST-SELLING AUTHOR

MILESTONES
INTERNATIONAL PUBLISHERS

Wired for Success, Programmed for Failure

ISBN: 978-1-935870-00-5
UPC: 88571300070-3

Printed in the United States of America.

© 2010 by Dr. James B. Richards

MileStones International Publishers
PO Box 104, Newburg, PA 17240
303.503.7257; Fax: 717.477.2261
www.milestonesintl.com

1 2 3 4 5 6 7 8 9 10 / 15 14 13 12 11

CONTENTS

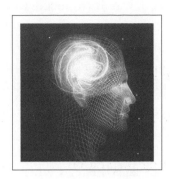

INTRODUCTION

I STEPPED OFF OF THE stage after motivating people to believe for the very best life has to offer, to find myself being confronted by a musician who was part of the program. What I didn't know was that his in-laws had just suffered terrible loss. The unfortunate turn of events had hurt him deeply and he was still in a reactionary mindset. As with most people who are reactionary, in order to protect what they do not understand they must fight against what they do not believe.

Before I had the opportunity to say anything, he was "in my face" launching a reasonably controlled but deliberate attack. "I'd like to see you sell this to people in third world countries who are starving!" he blasted. After a five-minute tirade I was finally able to respond, "I *have* shared this in third world countries—and it worked!"

Two things about success that we must realize are first, the principles of success are immutable, and second, success is relative. Immutable laws work anywhere with anyone, anytime! Although there are many relative factors that affect the application, the laws are absolute. No two people facing the same situation share all the same factors. There are always variables. Those variables do not change the destination, however; they only change the journey!

The principles of success are immutable.

I shared the following story with my upset friend. Several years ago while working in Mexico, I was introduced to a family that lived in a drainage pipe just outside the compound where I was lodging. They had small children and lived in deplorable lack. They attended one of the conferences conducted in the small village aimed at people living in destitute situations. One of my topics was success and prosperity.

The greatest injustice I could have done to that family was to look at their circumstances and withhold the truth that could change their world. I knew they would be challenged. I knew their ego would be touched. But I also knew that every man faces his ego when confronting the confines of the life for which he has settled. But I was confident in the power of the truth that, when believed in the human heart, will transform any person in any situation. When we feel we have something that will help people and then withhold it because of the magnitude of their need, it is only evidence that we really don't believe what we are saying.

> *When we feel we have something that will help people and then withhold it because of the magnitude of their need, it is only evidence that we really don't believe what we are saying.*

Some might argue, "Do you realize how offensive it would be to tell people in lack they could have a better life?" Of course I do! But I also realize it is wrong thinking, based on destructive beliefs, that is actually holding those people in their current circumstance. They have accepted and possibly become comfortable believing a lie. They settled for what they have when they didn't know what to do because settling is a coping mechanism that frees people from the conscious stress of their situation. Once people have settled, they have to defend their position to keep from resurrecting the conscious awareness of stress. People are offended when faced with the truth that challenges what they have accepted. But, as I discovered many years ago, the truth that has the most potential to set us free also has the most potential to offend!

Einstein said, "No problem can be solved from the same level of consciousness that created it." To put that into my own euphemism, "The thinking that got you into your problem will never get you out!" People think the way they do because they believe it is right. Being challenged with the possibility that they could change the very circumstances they have accepted initiates the defense mechanism to protect their ego by proving they are right! It is more important to justify circumstances than to discover solutions when ego is the driving motivation. That's when offense occurs. But the truth that offends one may set thousands free.

> *"The thinking that got you into your problem will never get you out!"*

Some months later when I returned to Mexico, the family in the drainage pipe had a chicken. This was a huge improvement over their previous circumstances. The next time I visited they had a chicken and a goat. Now their family was eating fresh eggs and goat's milk. While that doesn't seem monumental compared to our standard of living, it was relative prosperity compared to where they started and to the standard of living of the people around them. I don't know where they ended, but I do know they progressed continually as their mindset changed and they exchanged the lie for the truth.

I have seen these truths work for people from all walks of life, many different nations and all manner of circumstances. I have seen moderately successful business people become millionaires in a relatively short time. I have seen people go from barely getting by to having more than enough. Their definition of success was relative to where they started. But there is always one common denominator in those who make this journey. It is never the external sources that determine our ceiling for success; it is always how we have been programmed, what we have been led to believe by the influences around us.

Whether you are completely broke, moderately successful or multiplying your millions, these principles apply to you and these tools can be used by you. You will use the same tools no matter where you are in life.

Throughout this book your programming will be confronted! You will find yourself tempted to defend the very thinking that is holding you hostage to your current level of success or lack.

You cannot be both receptive and defensive; one precludes the other. You don't have to accept everything at face value but you do have to be willing to study, think, ponder and consider the possibility of the things you read herein. But more than anything else, you have to start any search with the willingness to find what you do not have. You have to attempt to open every door with a commitment to walk through it. You have to be willing to give up what you've got in order to find something better!

You have to be willing to give up what you've got in order to find something better!

I encourage you to write that statement on a card and use it for a book marker. Read it every time you open this book. The level to which you feel defensive and threatened is in exact proportion to the degree your life will change by this truth!

CHAPTER 1

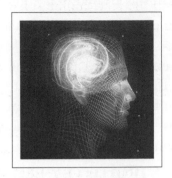

WIRED FOR SUCCESS

*Lack is an illusionary prison fortified
by the imaginary bars of our beliefs.*

M AN WAS NEVER DESIGNED to live in failure or lack. Failure and lack go against every inherent instinct in man. No matter how hard life is, there is a constant struggle in man to somehow make it better. We all want the best for our children. We want to provide for our family. Failure may have been something with which we have learned to cope, but it will never be *natural* (consistent with our original nature). In fact, coping with failure creates unrecognized systemic stress that robs us of the creativity and energy that could be mustered to bring about our desired success.

If you believe the biblical account of creation, which I do, then you too realize that man lived in abundance from the moment he awakened on planet Earth. Success and abundance are his natural state. He was wired for success from his first breath! Any other state is foreign, stressful and destructive! Man was placed in a garden with every need met and an unlimited supply of natural resources. He lived in the epitome of abundance. There was always more than enough. The result was that man lived free from the stress that occurs when having to face the daily struggle of meeting basic needs. Man was created to live in paradise!

Many are quick to point out the fall of man and its ensuing consequences as an explanation for the current struggle with success. Some even falsely believe that poverty and lack have some intrinsic value to man's personal development. The Bible is a testament to the fallacy of such irrational logic. From the fall forward God is not only reassuring man of His desire for his success and well-being, but also giving man a constant prescription for success in a world that has gone awry.

CONTROLLED BY BELIEFS

Failure and lack were foreign to man as he was originally designed but they became the "new normal" for man as he has been culturally programmed. Among the many freedoms we have is the freedom of belief and choice. Our beliefs become our subconscious programming that not only directs our life but also controls our capacity for understanding and perception. If we believe life should be hard, then we will experience a hard life. If success, in our paradigm, only belongs to the deserving, then we hold ourselves to a level of prosperity we feel we deserve. In other words, our beliefs become our choices.

Our beliefs become our choices.

The real problem is not as simple as "we live what we believe." The deeper issue is that our perception and our ability to understand are also limited to our beliefs. We see what confirms our beliefs no matter what the reality. Our capacity to enjoy abundance is hedged in by a lack of understanding that has nothing to do with our intellectual prowess. Our beliefs render us incapable of connecting the dots on the information that we know. As a result changing the world we perceive seems like an impossibility! Our perception and understanding limit the scope of our choices. We are always making the best possible choice with our current level of understanding. But beliefs, understanding and perception make us feel the choices are very limited. Our perception and understanding then keep us enslaved to the world we believe.

Scientists are now discovering a new world in cellular biology. Cutting-edge science is bringing the scientific and medical communities closer and closer to the biblical accounts of man, creation and nature. In the book, *The Healing Code*, Doctors Ben Johnson and Alex Lloyd point out that cellular memory include not only our personal memories, but also the memories of our genealogy.[1] This would mean that since I was created in the likeness and image of God, I would be genetically wired to function like my Creator. However, since my ancestors have lived lives that may have been filled with hardship, I have also come to be programmed to accept hardship as a way of life. The struggle for fulfilling my created potential goes beyond simple belief. It goes to the core of my being, my cellular programming!

Man has ultimate dominion of planet Earth. He is at the top of the intellectual hierarchy. In all of creation he is second only to the Creator! We were created in the likeness and image of God. There is nothing about God that says failure! There is nothing about the way our bodies work that says failure. Everything in us strives toward life, love and success! We, unlike any other creature on this planet, have the ability to change the quality of our life by changing our beliefs and decisions! Our dilemma lies in the deepest internal conflict imaginable. We have been wired for success—living in God's image and walking in His divine characteristics—but we have been programmed for failure! Nearly everything in this life has led us to believe success should be hard and only belongs to the precious few. Our beliefs become the force that guides, empowers or disempowers our life.

The struggle for fulfilling our created potential goes back to our cellular programming!

13

DESIGNED FOR SUCCESS

The success for which we were designed begins with recognizing the Creator as our source for optimum success and unlimited wisdom! Abundance is His desire for us; it was His expressed intention from the beginning and is still His goal for man. From these beliefs we simply harmonize ourselves with the will and wisdom of the Creator and find ourselves in a natural flow of success and creativity!

The person who does not believe success to be God's plan for man is placed in a tormenting dichotomy. Something deep in his being stirs his desire for success; he is always searching to make his life better, yet he feels there is something wrong, perverted or selfish about the desire to succeed and prosper. He is either bound to pursue success with great trepidation or to accept lack and limitation as normal. Many seeking to cope with the self-induced guilt abandon God as a way to cope with their need to succeed. Others resign themselves to a life of lack to appease the false sense of religious obligation!

Neither of those alternatives is acceptable. This book is designed to answer your questions about the limitations you have placed on your success and to show you how to move the boundaries within which you have lived. This is not a book just for Christians; it is for all people. The principles in this book have been proven in my own life and in the lives of those I have studied. These principles have been used for believers and non-believers alike for thousands of years. Because the laws of success are inalienable, they are available to all who will access them. But for those who struggle to free their minds and escape the prison of religious negativity I share this scripture: *"...it is He who gives you power to get wealth...."*[2]

The laws of success are available to all who will access them.

God Himself gives the power, the capacity and the strength to get wealth. It is part of His design for man, in this earth, to prosper and be successful. In fact, we are limited in the meaningful endeavors we can do in planet Earth if we are living in lack.

The days in which we live could well introduce us to times of potential hardship beyond what most people have ever seen. Yet, it is well within our capacity to turn the tide and reshape the future. However, the future must be reshaped by those who know, believe and live in true success and abundance. The success you will learn in this book is a success that doesn't make one man suffer so another man can succeed. It is a success that has the potential to create wealth for the entire planet. It is a wealth and success that emerges from the heart that influences everything in its realm for good.

The programming with which you struggle at this moment on some level is the same programming that leads to bad governmental financial policies, selfish bosses, the need for control and the idea that the world is collapsing. The world's economy is not at the root of what is collapsing. Rather, it is the heart of men who, through their programming, have no capacity for true success. If we will believe the truth and learn to succeed, then we can provide an answer for a world headed toward ruin. We can turn the tide!

In this book you will be shown how to reprogram your heart so you can function the way you were wired to function: with success, peace and joy! You will be introduced to a new concept of positive internal success. You will be empowered to succeed beyond your limiting circumstances or a past cluttered with reminders of failure. You will enjoy a success that contributes to every aspect of your life.

CHAPTER 2

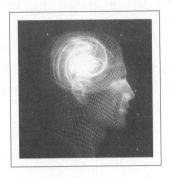

REDEFINING SUCCESS

*Definitions are predetermined destinations that force our life's
course along paths we did not choose!*

IN OUR PURSUIT OF success it is essential that we start by defining what *we* actually mean when we say the word *success!* Definitions are not mere intellectual terminology. Definitions are part of our heart's belief system. They are intimately connected to and deeply interwoven with our sense of self! And equally important, they are a part of our cultural programming. Success, like prosperity, is a subjective concept. It can mean many different things to many different people and can vary from culture to culture. Our culture gave us a definition of success long before we ever considered its meaning. In other words, someone else chose our definitions, thereby programming our destination.

MY DEFINITION OF SUCCESS

Success for me, after growing up in abject poverty, came to mean just getting by. Just getting by meant I could usually get to the bank in time to cover the bad checks I had written for groceries the day before payday. It meant I could get to the utility company just before my utilities were turned off. It meant that every extra dollar that came in would get there just in time for some unforeseen disaster that would once again leave me penniless. But all that was all right because I still paid my bills and managed to get by! And based on my definition of success, that was as good as it could get…for me!

Although God wired me for success, my upbringing programmed me for failure. But even worse, my culture forced me to accept a perverted definition of success that could have held me in poverty and lack all of my life. Then to seal the deal, my early religious programming reinforced my corrupt definition!

Our internal definition of success creates a map with a course and a destination that we may not have actually charted ourselves! I didn't really deliberately, intellectually, accept my definition of success. My mother worked hard, as a single parent in the early 1950s, to raise three children on a salary of $19 per week! I loved and respected her for all of her sacrifices. I never would have considered her efforts to have been a failure. So by default they became my concept of success.

Through the years I may have made a lot more money. But by definition my experience of success never changed. No matter how much I made, I always *just got by*. It was like working hard and putting my money in pockets with holes. Actually, in the mid-1960s I made really good money. I worked as a boilermaker during the day. I also played in a band on the weekends, and I built, swapped and sold musical instruments during the week. I made great money. But I always found myself just getting by.

Because I had this corrupt definition of success, the destination was chosen. *Just getting by* was where I was going to go no matter how I charted my course. You may choose any number of routes to get to your vacation location. Regardless, however, of the route you choose, your map will only take you to the destination of your choice. The scenery is different. The time it takes to get there may vary. But in the end, you are still at the destination you chose.

I know you may be saying, "I never chose this destination!" Actually, you did. In fact, every condition that determines the quality of your life was chosen at some point. It may have been unconsciously chosen. It may have been chosen by default, pressure or persuasion, but it was chosen! Before you get embarrassed and defensive you need to see the upside of this. If you chose the quality of life you now have and it happened, then you can choose a better quality of life and expect it to happen!

BELIEFS ARE OUR THERMOSTAT

Beliefs of the heart create our quality of life. People may momentarily rise above their beliefs or sink beneath their beliefs, but they will always return to the level of their beliefs. Beliefs are like a thermostat. They monitor our life just like a thermostat monitors the temperature. Any change in our quality of life will be allowed up to a certain extent. But if we move too far from our core beliefs the heart sends signals to our brain, our body and our environment to bring things back to the current setting! The invisible boundaries that we encounter over and over are not really "out there." They are "in here"! Nothing will change to any sustainable degree until we learn to reset the thermostat— our heart's beliefs.

If you chose the quality of life you now have and it happened, then you can choose a better quality of life and expect it to happen!

Some people say we form our life paradigm, our core beliefs, by the time we are five years of age. This means that before I was old enough to speak or intellectually think, I had pretty much forged my sense of self, which determines my life experiences. Beliefs can be forged many different ways. Circumstance, self-talk, repetition and emotional experiences all become a part of developing our beliefs. Once beliefs are established they become the substructure of our subconscious thoughts and feelings.

Beliefs are different from thoughts. Thoughts are short-term. Thoughts occur because of what we choose to think about. Thoughts have the ability to create emotions. Emotions are also short-term. They tend to last as long as we have our thoughts focused or until we focus on a new thought. This is why positive thinking fails to bring long-lasting change for most people. It only works as long as we can control our thoughts. (According to studies we hold our thoughts for an incredibly short period.)

> *Beliefs generate our prevailing, subconscious thoughts that emerge effortlessly to direct and control our lives.*

Beliefs, however, are quite different. Beliefs are long-term. They generate our prevailing, subconscious thoughts that emerge effortlessly to direct and control our life. While intellectual thoughts create short-term emotions, beliefs give rise to long-term feelings. Feelings are abiding! They are a reflection of our sense of self. Our subconscious thoughts and long-term feelings require no effort; they simply emerge when we are not consciously focused.

It is this very dichotomy that creates most of the stress in our lives. This seemingly irresolvable conflict between what we intellectually desire and choose and what we are subconsciously guided to do is the perfect example of the person who keeps charting a new course because of his intellectual desires yet arrives at the same old destination because of his definitions! No matter how many times we say we want to be more successful, if our definition of success does not change we will get exactly what we say: more of our current definition of success.

CHANGING MY BELIEFS

I was raised poor. Everyone in my neighborhood was poor. Most of my friends were poor. As an adult I gave my life to the Lord and in many areas of my life I started over brand-new. I knew drugs were destructive and the message I heard at church supported that, so I was able to work through the beliefs that had led me to be a substance abuser. One after another, I received reinforcement for my choice to repent (change my thoughts and beliefs) about destructive behaviors.

However, the church I was attending very subtly reinforced my corrupt beliefs about success. Salvation is supposed to be a place of starting over, of redefining and charting an entirely new course. For that to happen, however, we must be willing to examine our *every belief* and bring it into harmony with God's plan for our lives. From the day I came to Jesus to now, I have been willing to question the source of everything I believe. This is the only way I can be assured that I am living in the beliefs I have chosen!

Sadly, my early church experience seemed to support the idea that wanting more than enough to get by was carnal and selfish! This served to solidify a destructive belief that made it more unlikely that I ever would break free of that belief! Now I thought God supported my definition. I mistakenly thought the voice of the church and the voice of God were one and the same! As adults, few things in life influence our beliefs as much as what we are taught at church. Sadly, much of what we are taught at church takes us deeper into bondage instead of freeing us to make new healthy choices.

I spent the next eight years living out my belief. No matter how bad things got, I always got by. But no matter how good things went, I still just got by. I was able to look at the hard times that I had come through and find a false solace for my internal conflict. But I was growing weary of working hard and still living under the pressure of *just getting by!* What I didn't realize was my internal thermostat, my heart, would have to create sickness, hardship and crippling circumstances to rein me back in every time I ventured very far beyond my heart definition of success.

There is an old proverb that says, "When the student is ready the teacher appears." I got ready, but not because I was willing to face myself. I was launched into opening my heart when after several years of sickness and incredible medical bills and *just getting by* my wife gave me an awakening. One day my wife and I sat down to a meal. As was our custom, we gave thanks. As I thanked God for this provision, I also thanked Him that every need was met! At that moment my wife slapped her hand on the table and said, "I'm tired of just having our needs met. I don't think this is how God wants us to live."

Inwardly a barrage of emotions sought to explode from my mouth in a detonation of defensiveness. But as I sought to understand the depth of my emotions and why her reaction so offended me, I had to admit that more than anything else my male ego was hurt. It was excruciating to face the fact that I was not providing for my family as I desired to do. I was embarrassed!

Excuses only make you feel comfortable staying where you are.

My mind quickly raced to justify itself. I had been seriously ill for a number of years. "It wasn't my fault we were broke!" In other words, I had good excuses for our current condition. But excuses never serve to make anything better. They only serve to make you feel comfortable staying where you are!

My deep love for my wife was a stronger motivating factor than my need to justify myself. My desire to take care of my family made me question what had been my "normal" for so many years. Over the next few months—because I was now ready—tapes and books fell into my hands that answered many of my questions. How I read the Bible changed. I found answers and promises that had long eluded me. My eyes had not seen them; my heart had not understood them. I had closed my mind so I would not have to question what I had accepted as true. But now I saw!

One of the key realities that caused me to redefine my definition of success came from someone who pointed out that there was no one more selfish than the person who just wanted to get by. If I was just getting by then I had nothing to contribute to the world. I had no means to make the world a better place. I could not feed the hungry or create jobs. I realized that there was a false security in my corrupt definition of success. It fed a self-justified "stinginess." It kept me from facing my fears of success. But mostly it masked my fear of trusting God for a life bigger than my culture had defined!

In a very short period of time, as I daily worked on these beliefs, my world, my prosperity and my opportunity grew as my heart grew! I never sought external success. I merely renewed my sense of self as it related to success and prosperity. As my heart changed, my opportunities changed. The way I responded to opportunities moved me from the just-getting-by stage to a world with no boundaries!

CHAPTER 3

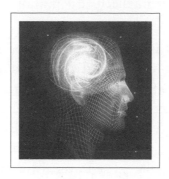

HOLISTIC SUCCESS

Money can corrupt but true success can only
contribute to a better quality of life.

F OR SOME, SUCCESS IS a goal rather than a state. That which is seen as a goal is worked for and earned. And it can be held only by continued labor that sustains the current definition. That which is a state, however, is about "being." When success is about being it always leads to "healthy doing." But success based on doing will never become being. Therefore, it is a labor that has no end and a struggle that has no rest!

"Being" works from the inside out. It is about who you are; it is your identity! Doing is an attempt to work from the outside in. There is the false idea that reaching the goal will create the desired sense of self that makes you feel successful. Unfortunately, that which comes from the outside only temporarily stimulates our five senses. And like all stimulation, you need more and bigger to sustain the initial feeling! That which makes you feel successful today will not suffice tomorrow.

Success as a goal can be somewhat compartmentalized. In fact, success as a goal means it is something you work to have. Therefore, while in the process of working in the area that would create your success you can create massive failure in other parts of your life. The conscious mind, which is the basis of our intellectual definitions, can only focus on one thing at a time!

When people find success by developing a healthy identity in their relationship with God it brings about what I call holistic success. Holistic success is a success that affects every area of our life in a healthy, positive manner. Instead of neglecting other areas to pursue a single area, all aspects of life are developed simultaneously. In holistic success the main objective is to live a life congruent with our sense of self. That which violates our sense of self is naturally passed over for a more compatible option. Success that emerges from our sense of self will never violate the other valued parts of our life!

THE PROBLEM WITH COMPARTMENTALIZED SUCCESS

The Bible says, *"The love of money is the root of all kinds of evil."*[1] Some who are very loose with the Word of God have twisted that to say money itself is the root of evil. Money is a neutral power. Like so many things in planet Earth, it is neither good nor bad of itself. We forget that the Bible also says, *"To the pure all things are pure and to the evil all things are evil."*[2] We make money and all other created things good or bad based on how we use them.

Money becomes good or evil based on the heart of the person interacting with it. In fact, you don't actually need to "have" money for it to corrupt you. Just the desire for it can destroy you if that desire comes from a destructive definition (belief). Conversely, the lack of money can destroy you. With money it's all about what kind of expectations you project onto it, why you want it, how you use it and what you believe about it!

The wisest, richest man in the world said, *"The prosperity of fools shall destroy them."*[3] A sure road to a life of destruction can be to pursue money apart from developing your own heart in the process. When money is your measurement of success, you can be assured that the more money you get the more problems you will have. Having money apart from a healthy, biblically based sense of self-worth will magnify and multiply your every flaw, your every selfishness and your every ego problem!

If having money is your definition or proof of success, it will take the top priority in your life because mankind is wired to be and feel successful. When your definition of success is skewed it will take priority above your spouse, above your children, above your health and above your God! Of course you will never admit it and may not even realize it. All the time you're spending away from home, you will insist it is

> *When money is your measurement of success, you can be assured that the more money you get the more problems you will have.*

for the family you never see, the spouse you're neglecting and the children you aren't really raising!

Most of us have been taught a concept of success based on a hierarchy of commitment: God first, then our family, then church, then our job and then whatever you believe should be next. The problem with this concept is it always means you are neglecting one thing to pursue another. Some area is always sacrificing for some other area to succeed.

The process leads to a near schizophrenic lifestyle. We get fully committed to God. So we are doing all the things that we believe prove our commitment. While we are doing that, we realize we are neglecting our family. That can be met with a response of guilt or even anger. So, we naturally go to the aid of our family. Then, of course, we feel guilt about abandoning God. Then, we get pressure from work. We want to provide for our family so we have to focus on work. Now we feel guilty about neglecting God, family and church! There is no place of peace for the vertical hierarchical concept of success and commitment! It is full of conflicts and contradictions. Every success is mixed with a failure in some area!

When one area of our life makes us feel like a failure, there is a likelihood that we will give ourselves to the place where we feel like a success and avoid those places where we feel like a failure. This is a road to divorce to save the job that we defended with the self-deception, "I'm doing all this for my family!"

HOW ARE YOU THINKING?

In holistic success I am not doing to become; I am, therefore I do! But holistic success will not be actualized by simply comprehending an idea. We know that when people think from a place of identity it actually activates different parts of their brain. The parts of the brain that are activated reflect when people are listening to their heart or to their intellectual mind. When there is an awareness of identity all decisions are made in a way that supports one's sense of self. On the other hand, when people make decisions with no sense of self, the part of their brain that is activated is more about survival. In the survival mode, the mind hardens to the heart and closes out its life-giving wisdom and direction. In other words, I can act in a way that totally violates my sense of self if I am not open to my sense of self (heart).

The brain-heart relationship in decision-making is much like the functioning of the physical body. When we function from a place of stress (our head) the blood does not heal or nurture the internal organs. Instead it is moved out to the limbs to prepare for fight or flight. Our immune function, which is normally on the watch to protect us from predators, does not function as it should. The organs then become vulnerable to all manner of disease.

Likewise, when we think apart from a sense of identity (the heart) we think from survival (carnal mind), which gives rise to every negative motivation and a fear-based decision-making process. Our decisions are driven by the fear of destruction instead of the "wired in" capacity to succeed. The selfish basis from which we make our decisions creates failures and stresses in those areas we are neglecting. We deny all that we are as *beings* and justify it! Emotional survival is about the survival of the ego. It is the epitome of "living for self"! It brings out the worst in all people.

We must realize that the compartmentalized concepts of the brain have no capacity for the identity factors of the heart. When success is independent of our identity it will always come at the cost of some other area of our life that we value. What happens in the physical to the parts of the body is mirrored in the parts of our life. The natural mind (the brain) tells us, "All this is too much to keep up with. It's too complicated. How will you ever be able to think about who you are while you're making important financial decisions?" The truth is, we can't, if we rely on our brain. But when a chosen identity is written on our heart it emerges effortless and becomes the window through which we interpret the entire world and the perspective from which all decisions are made.

> ### *When success is independent of our identity it will always come at the cost of some other area of our life that we value.*

Most people have never decided who they want to be. Something I recommend for all people to do is write a character sketch of who you want to be. It can be up to three pages. Describe the "you" with all the character traits you desire, the way you will treat people and how you will live in success. Write it all out in the first person, present tense as if it is already a reality. Use phrases like, "this is how I feel" and "this is how I treat people." None of it is about who you hope to be. It is about who you are! I also suggest that you include all the fruit of the Spirit: love, joy, peace, longsuffering, kindness, goodness, faithfulness, gentleness and self-control. This provides your left brain with a rational, biblical basis to have confidence.

Read your character sketch every morning. You may even find that you need to read it during the day, but you also should read it the last thing every night. As this becomes your sense of self, your heart will guide you into a lifestyle that always sustains who you see yourself to be. When your primary goal is to survive, to save your ego, you can never thrive. However, as long as you are nurturing who you are, you will not only survive but you also will thrive.

CHAPTER 4

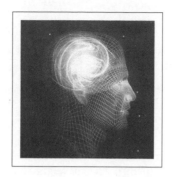

A WORLD OF ABUNDANCE

*Abundance hinges on our capacity to see opportunity
where others see disaster.*

THERE ARE MANY FACTORS that can undermine your belief in personal abundance. Among the most deadly is the feeling of lack. The feeling of lack can emerge from many subtle sources. It can come from how you were raised. It can be a projection of your sense of self onto the world around you. Among Americans today the feeling of lack is almost unavoidable. The repeated false messages from politicians and the news media put everyone at risk of succumbing to an all-pervasive feeling of doom!

This is not intended to be a political rant, but be assured that those who create massive wealth are not duped by the media or the political world. It really doesn't matter which political party we are for or against; they all have played the same game for years. They have created a false sense of lack as a way to tax, control the masses and reward their contributors. Then, the media is more than willing to create hysteria for the sake of ratings. Bad news is big money and high ratings! Our problem is that we are mesmerized by the continual flow of emotionally charged information. But worst of all, we don't know who to trust!

Two factors always involved in programming the heart are information plus emotion.

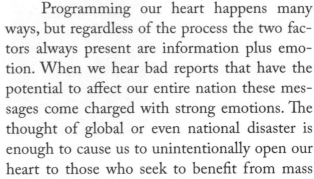

Programming our heart happens many ways, but regardless of the process the two factors always present are information plus emotion. When we hear bad reports that have the potential to affect our entire nation these messages come charged with strong emotions. The thought of global or even national disaster is enough to cause us to unintentionally open our heart to those who seek to benefit from mass fear and uncertainty. Combine that with the repetition of morning, evening and 24-hour news casting, and we have the greatest influencers in the world programming our beliefs and expectations. Only those who know how to guard their hearts are immune to such epic programming.

THE EARTH IS NOT LACKING

Your first step toward recovering yourself from this deluge of despair is to know the truth. From the beginning of time, planet Earth has supplied super-abundantly for its inhabitants. I can fully assure you that there are more than enough natural resources to sustain all of humanity for many lifetimes at a standard of living better than anything the world has ever seen. Only in recent years have we begun to hear messages of shortages. The *threats*, not the reality, of global warming, energy shortages and uncontrollable phenomenon jeopardize not only our prosperity but also our existence.

There are more than enough natural resources to sustain all of humanity for many lifetimes at a standard of living better than anything the world has ever seen.

Few things make us as susceptible to control as feelings of lack. When we feel inadequate, incapable or inferior we are vulnerable. Preachers, politicians and salespeople seek to create a need before offering us their solution to the feeling of lack they just created by their "pitch." As we buy into the deception of those who seek to benefit from our need, we gladly give up our dreams for a false sense of security that meets our need for survival.

But those messages come from people who work diabolical conspiracies to control the world through a false sense of lack. Throughout history those who were aware of the abundance held the rest of the population captive through misinformation! This same misinformation is multiplied through the mainline media in such a way that it seems only a complete fool would question it. And while the average man is consumed with fear and pessimism the rich keep getting richer through taxation and overpricing of goods.

We live in a day when the merchants of mayhem, in the name of saving planet Earth, are shouting false warnings about the impending lack facing our nation. If there is lack, it is not because of a depletion of natural resources. It is only a man-made lack created to control the markets and minds of the world!

The ultra-wealthy have complete confidence in the resources of the world. That is why they continue to invest billions of dollars each year into exploration and development. They know the greatest wealth is yet to be found. There are more than enough natural resources in America for us to live abundant lives and to experience greater wealth and affluence than we have ever known. The American dream is not dead, but it is buried alive!

For us to face the future with the hope of success we must never buy into the idea that we are out of resources. Our Creator did not make planet Earth to run out before we have finished the course.

AMERICA HAS PLENTY!

One of the greatest misinformation programs is about oil. In the absence of oil, "they" say, without a suitable alternative, America's commerce and opportunity would grind to a snail's pace, launching us into a pre-industrial world. If that did happen, be assured that those who have a heart for success would find a way to excel in any environment, whether real or man-made. But it is essential that you know *there is no lack of oil!* The following are just two of dozens of articles that have come out over the past few years confirming the incredible reserves available in America.

At AmericanFreePress.net, Pat Shannan reports:

It has been more than a year since the Department of Interior announced that North Dakota and Montana have an estimated 3 to 4.3 billion barrels of recoverable oil in an area known as the Bakken Formation, but little is being done about it.[1]

In a *Newsweek* article on July 14, 2008, entitled "America's Untapped Oil," Jim Moskou writes:

Could the Rockies out-produce Saudi Arabia? Royal Dutch Shell, the international oil giant, thinks the solution to America's oil crisis may lie in the heart of Colorado. Since 1981, the company has quietly funded a multimillion dollar research project that many call a quest for energy's Holy Grail. The mission: to discover a way to safely and economically extract fuel from oil shale, a type of sedimentary rock found in Wyoming, Utah, and especially Colorado's Western Slope. The potential windfall is staggering. Studies over the years by industry and government alike estimate that there may be between 800 billion and more than one trillion barrels of oil locked up in these rocks—nearly three times the known reserves in Saudi Arabia. **That would be enough oil to supply America for the next 400 years.**

Coal is another essential natural resource for American industry and future opportunity. The primary use for coal is creating electricity.

Clean-energy.us reports on the status of coal reserves in America provide this stunning information:

> The United States has enormous coal "resources" and "recoverable reserves." The most reliable information about coal is published by the Energy Information Administration (EIA). The most recent figures available from the EIA, show that America's estimated recoverable reserves of coal —
>
> - Stand at 275 billion tons, an amount that is greater than any other nation in the world.
> - Are capable of meeting domestic demand for more than 250 years at current rates of consumption.[2]

The same could be said for natural and other resources. There are more than enough conventional sources of energy in America for us to go on recklessly using what we have for many lifetimes. Or, we could peacefully and confidently use the time to develop alternative resources that would be good for our planet, better for our health and helpful in stimulating the economy. Plus there is always the alternative of nuclear power. And then there is the abundance of wind, sun, magnetic and other sources of power.

There are more than enough conventional sources of energy in America for us to go on recklessly using what we have for many lifetimes.

As politically incorrect as it is to do so, we must momentarily address global warming. I live in Huntsville, Alabama, in what would be considered by some to be the home of NASA and a pool of scientists who know more about our solar system than possibly any other group of people in the world. The consensus among those whom I talk to is that global warming is most likely the result of sunspot activity and has nothing or little to do with man's environmental pollution.

I am not in favor of pollution. Neither am I in favor of wasting our natural resources. But when there are no facts to support the political position of global warming, new studies indicate the previous material was incorrect and the weather cannot be accurately predicted for my weekend barbecue, I find it hard to believe that scientists can accurately predict what will happen for the next hundred years! Unfortunately, it is so politically incorrect to oppose the current interpretation of global warming that scientists would lose their jobs if they stood up and told what they know. (By the way, political correctness is the manipulation of the powers that be who seek to intimidate you into not thinking logically while shaping your thinking and beliefs to fulfill their will.)

WHICH DO YOU SEE?

Reading this material can be incredibly depressing or incredibly uplifting. But at this moment you can make of it only what your heart has the capacity to perceive. I choose to see opportunity. After all, if I succumb to those who seek to control my beliefs I will never create the resources to influence and educate the world. Believing the lie creates a self-fulfilling prophecy fueled by my inability to respond optimistically.

The stress of these reports is devastating to our ability to think positively and creatively. New studies indicate that when we are overcome with negative feelings the brain takes over and attempts to create survival strategies. We stop listening to the heart. A healthy heart tries to take us to success but our brain only thinks of survival. The path of survival and success cannot be traveled at the same time unless led by the heart. When thinking with the mind, it is one or the other!

The Chinese character that most closely represents stress has two meanings: danger and opportunity. Such is life...that which could push us into "fight or flight" and rob us of virtually all creative thinking could also open our eyes to the opportunities that exist in an environment others would consider threatening. It is the beliefs of our heart that determine which one we shall see.

If your heart is overcome by the condition of the world, the cure is not to fix the world. I'm not implying that we shouldn't do what we can. But fixing the world is a task so big that once again you find yourself overwhelmed by the state of things beyond your control. Whether creating wealth or finding happiness, those "who know," know that these are matters of the heart. You cannot influence anything for good outside of you without first influencing your own heart for good.

> ### *You cannot influence anything for good outside of you without first influencing your own heart for good.*

The world is full of natural resources. It is also full of greedy, selfish people who seek to become richer through disinformation. Only what you believe about you, in your heart, can turn this threatening situation into an opportunity to find greater success. By establishing your heart you become immovable in the face of those who seek to take you captive through fear. But even more, you stay creative and optimistic while others hide their heads in the sand.

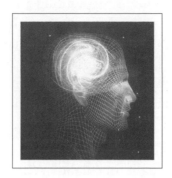

CHAPTER 5

THE CULTURAL TRANCE

*The wiser you are, the more options you see. Being in the will of
God should be a realm of limitless options!*

MOST OF THE WORLD is walking around in a trance. Their eyes are
wide open, they are making decisions and doing business, but
they are doing so from a perception that has only a limited basis
in reality. It is a culturally induced state that alters our perception and
experience of reality. When our perception is altered so is our sense of options. Options are the fundamental factor in our ability to live in freedom.
Freedom provides us with a wide scope of options. But to the very degree
we have been blinded to our options we have also lost our freedom.

In his groundbreaking research into hypnotism, Dr. John Kappas
made some astounding discoveries. The most powerful way to induce a
state of hypnotism is not to bring about relaxation, but to induce stress.
By inducing enough stress factors in what is called the induction, a person
will internally go into the fight or flight mode. The flight mode is a state
of high suggestibility, wherein it is easiest to influence a person's subconscious beliefs.

Contrary to what most people believe, hypnotism is not a trance-like state. Rather, it is a state of suggestibility. According to Dr. Kappas, hypnosis is created by an overload of message units, thus disorganizing our inhibitory process (critical mind), triggering our fight/flight mechanism and ultimately creating a hyper-suggestible state, which provides access to the subconscious mind. Every person who has encountered extreme stress has, by default, become suggestible—that is, hypnotized.[1]

Hypnotism is not a trance-like state. Rather, it is a state of suggestibility.

When we enter the fight or flight mode our environment has much to do with how we will express that "fight" or "flight." When we are in environments we trust or environments over which we feel we have no control flight may not mean we run externally. Rather, it may mean that we retreat inwardly, from our views and opinions. Thus we become suggestible to the input of the stimuli in our environment.

As children, up until somewhere around the age of 11 or 12, we are constantly in a state that makes us very suggestible to the input from our environment. Kids stay in the alpha state, which is identical to a relaxed meditative state, until around age 11 or 12, which makes them highly suggestible. As adults we have to put forth effort that causes us to return to the alpha state, where we retreat inwardly and open our subconscious mind to suggestions from our environment. When we were children we were being constantly programmed. We were creating our paradigm of life, self, success and all the other factors that relate to who we are and our existence.

Many different factors program us to establish our "life limits" for success. There is the genetic programming that occurs at birth. On some level we experience a degree of cellular memories based on our entire family tree. Then there is the pre-birth environment that makes impressions on us in part, at least, by our mother's perceptions and experiences of the world around her. Once we are conceived there are many other influencing factors. But possibly the three most powerful external forces that shape our beliefs about finances and success are our family, religion and government.

The degree of influence each would have is quite variable, based on many psychological factors. But be assured that much of what we accept as our "normal" was influenced by some combination of these three factors.

THE INFLUCENCE OF FAMILY

Family plays a major role in the success mindset for many people. In every case, it will be the model to which we comply or the standard we determine to overcome. How our family lives, what their average income is and how they view life can be a mold that is hard to escape. Yet, some people not only escape, but their view of their family is even reactionary, "I will never live like they live!" This intransigent response catapults many people to more success than any of their family members.

Although the family influence is incredibly powerful, it may be the easiest of the three to escape on superficial levels. To escape on a superficial level is when you force yourself to a better standard of living but never deal with the true issues of the heart, that is, the beliefs about you and who you are in relation to your family. There can be subtle but deep pervasive guilt about living better than your parents. There can be the feeling that rising above your parents' limiting views is somehow personally slanderous to them.

Although the pitfalls of breaking free from our family's influence are many, breaking free from the general family standard of living is the most common escape. Nurturing parents encourage their children to have more and go farther than they have gone. Healthy parents want their children to have a better education, a nicer house and make more money than they will ever make. This may be one of the primary reasons people break free from the family mold!

Dysfunctional controlling parents, however, are the ones most likely to hold their children back. Sometimes their very attempts at pushing them forward are the seeds of their failure. Parents who undermine the child's self-worth, whether intentionally or ignorantly, are programming that child to fail. Negative motivation such as criticism and nagging, which

41

are meant to push the child forward, can establish an array of personal limiting beliefs that undermine success in every area of life. Keep in mind that one enters a hypnotic state of suggestibility when enough stress is introduced to cause the person to enter the flight mode, making his or her subconscious vulnerable to suggestion. The parent's negative comments become subconscious suggestions that are accepted as true.

At this point we must note, however, that once a child reaches about 4 to 6 years old, his or her brain functions in the alpha state. Even though it is a state of heightened suggestibility, unlike earlier deeper states this is a state that requires one's willful participation. Therefore, at an age when they are most impressionable they are taking in everything that happens around them and creating life paradigms. They are mixing together judgments and interpretations with the emotions generated, which ultimately become their sense of reality and identity!

The heart is designed in such a way that you cannot be influenced by outside sources. Even in the Bible, aside from receiving a new heart at the born-again experience, you and only you are in control of the beliefs of your heart. Everything that happens to your heart will be by your choice. God ministers to your spirit and people around you minister to your soul, but then you take that input and say things, internally, that become the beliefs of the heart. Only you can write on, influence, guard, establish or minister to your heart!

Only you can write on, influence, guard, establish or minister to your heart!

Every hypnotist will tell you, "You are in control at all times. Nothing can happen to you that you do not choose." You can be assured that he or she is telling you the truth. The idea that anyone can make you believe something you do not want to believe or behave in a way you do not choose is just not true! So, if we are in control, then how is it that we are influenced by the things our parents say or the things that we see daily in our family environment?

The Bible tells us that when we judge, the measure we mete will determine what comes back to us.[2] In other words, the judgment I place on anything is the way it will affect me, or come back to me. Judgment has many subtle nuances, but more than anything it is when we assume to know why something is occurring. It doesn't matter if my judgment (the reason why) is correct or not. It affects me as if my judgment is correct.

For example, you may say, "We are poor because there are too many children." This can create a belief that makes you feel that you are a burden to the world. Or, it could make you believe that you could never be prosperous and have children. Once we determine the "why," the other embellishments determine how the judgment will affect us.

The judgments I reach about why my parents say what they say and live the way they live determines how it affects me. Sadly, most of our judgments place us at the center of the reason. In other words, the "why" has something to do with me! When I make anything about me, it has a multiplied capability of influencing my heart. If I over-identify with my family, then their standard becomes mine and their lot in life determines my lot in life.

But the two areas that present the most threatening aspects of emotional control are religion and government. These represent a power bigger than our father or mother. At least with our father or mother we can escape their control by growing up and leaving. Or, we can be fortunate enough to have nurturing parents. But government and religion are the arenas wherein we feel the least amount of control and therefore the least amount of options. The less control we feel we have in any situation, the more stress it creates. The more stress we experience, the less coherent and rational are our decisions. But we must remember that when there is sufficient stress we can become highly suggestible. When we become suggestible, the suggestion seems real. Then, coupled with our self-talk, we create feelings of powerlessness, thereby establishing limiting beliefs.

THE INFLUENCE OF RELIGION AND POLITICS

I am a committed believer and follower of the Lord Jesus and I am deeply patriotic, yet the two things I find most detestable and damnable are religion and politics. But remember, politics is as diametrically opposed to patriotism as religion is to Christianity. They are both self-serving systems of control for the greater good of the greedy elite. In each scenario one is designed to set you free while the other is designed to take your freedoms. Religion and politics use fear and deceit to move people to willfully give over the control of their life to those who will take all their freedoms to facilitate the progression of their own personal agendas.

Politics and religion create the feeling of lack and then offer to make you safe in exchange for some aspect of your freedom. The politicians make you feel there is no more opportunity and religion makes you believe that success and freedom are inherently evil. These are the two areas of life where we feel we can't change anything. After all, how can we change God (the version of God they taught us) and how can we change an entire nation? Even when the religious and the political offer us hope, it always comes with a price, some indebtedness that is created toward them.

Our struggle is never whether or not we believe; our struggle is what we believe.

Everything about our faith and the American way should create a sense of freedom and limitlessness. If that's not what is being inspired in you, it's time to listen to someone else. Jesus is the One who said, *"All things are possible to him who believes."*[3] The fear-mongers make us believe we are limited. They don't steal the actual possibility or opportunity…they steal the belief.

Belief is an interesting phenomenon. Faith believes what God says. Doubt believes the circumstances. Our struggle is never whether or not we believe; our struggle is what we believe. When something is believed our deep, abiding feelings and thoughts harmonize with the thing being believed. It is thought, perceived and felt, so it must be true! Our beliefs become the reality that we experience and create.

When considering success you have to ask yourself, "Do I *feel* like my dreams are possible?" Don't ask if you *think* they are possible. You can have an intellectual idea that you don't really believe. The key is what do you feel?

Sit quietly, calm yourself and breathe deeply for about ten breaths. Then state your goal or dream. Simply notice how you feel when you make the statement. Are your feelings positive? Does it feel possible? Does it feel good? Or do you feel uncomfortable? Do you start thinking of reasons you can't live your dream? Do you feel negative emotions? Or, most telling, do you start thinking of excuses or reasons you can't do what you have said? If you have negative feelings or rationalizations about your stated goal, then you are believing something besides *"All things are possible."*

Why is there conflict between what you want and what you think or feel? Simple! You've been hypnotized. Your cultural influences throughout life created stressors when they contradicted your dreams and goals. At some point you went inside yourself and started making judgments, justifications or some form of negative self-talk. However you did it, you agreed with the voices of limitation. They affected your deep feelings and you acquired a new belief. You may intellectually cling to learned information but actually *feel* something very different.

You may have escaped the circumstances and not the belief. You may have learned new information but never changed in your heart. You may have seen external change but you kept listening to the same sources telling you the same thing and influencing your deep feelings until that thing became entrenched in the beliefs of your heart and your cellular memories. Now everything in you is working to keep you within the boundaries of the beliefs you accepted. At this point in the struggle between thoughts and feelings, feelings always win!

But do not despair! You do not have to stay within the boundaries of your limiting beliefs. I will introduce you to heart tools that help you establish new boundaries that give you limitless options and opportunity.

The conflict will end when your thoughts and feelings harmonize with your true programming. You will enter the potential for limitless success!

CHAPTER 6

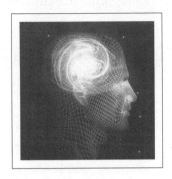

LEARNING TO FAIL

We live in the illusion of how we have learned to see ourselves. Regardless of what we have learned and how much it has negatively affected our life, we can learn something different!

OTIVATIONAL SPEAKER AND LIFE coach Tony Robbins says, "Practice doesn't make perfect, it makes permanent!"[1] Truer words may never have been spoken. Doing something over and over the wrong way doesn't make us better at it. It simply makes us better at doing it the wrong way! Similarly, we spend our lives being taught to think and feel inadequate, inferior and insecure. We are taught that success is deserved only when we work hard enough. We learn almost every wrong thing imaginable about success and prosperity. Our society is so permeated with wrong thinking that we are inundated with repetitious reminders that teach us to think for failure and accept it as the norm!

It takes a lifetime of practice to get good at failure. Why? It's because failure is not natural, it is learned! It is the result of a lifelong practice of thinking and doing things a certain way. It is completely unnatural, yet after years of practice it becomes an indelible imprint on the fabric of our nature. Failure is accepted as the "easy way" and success is considered the hard way. This upside-down thinking distorts our internal scale of pain and pleasure. It alters our perception of what causes pain and what brings pleasure.

Failure is not natural, it is learned!

Jesus said, *"You nullify the word of God by your tradition."*[2] The word *tradition* literally means that which is transmitted either orally or in writing.[3] Our culture is the product of that which has been accepted as fact and orally passed down to subsequent generations. After multiple generations of accepting information as fact, it becomes more powerful in our life than the Word of God! It becomes normal and familiar! Despite God's many promises to give us the *"power to get wealth,"* the inclusion of prosperity in the New Covenant and the grace of God to live in all that God has promised, our traditions that have been handed down influence us to believe something quite to the contrary.

We have learned to make success hard. We have learned to fear success. In some circles we have learned to reject success as evil! Suffering and lack is considered by some to be a godly trait! A lifetime of programming creates beliefs and boundaries in our heart that seem insurmountable. We live in the illusion that it would take monumental amounts of faith to scale the wall of prosperity and sip from its golden chalice.

Not only is failure learned, but all of the negative thoughts and emotions that support failure are learned! They have been programmed into us by a lifetime of words, models and thoughts. We learned to feel the way we feel about life. Someone taught us how to feel about success. It was even imposed on us how we should feel about ourselves! The idea that life should be hard, success should be difficult and we should strive for our dreams is a violation of the very dignity and worth with which we were crowned from the beginning of creation!

PROGRAMMING OUR CELLS

As new medical insights emerge, we are gaining incredible revelation about how we develop both physically and emotionally. At the time of conception we start with a basic blueprint that is some combination of our mother and father. It is as if all of their life experiences, right up to their particular emotions at the moment of conception, are programmed into our cells. That is our starting life blueprint!

At one time it was thought that basic DNA programming was the end-all to our life programming. It was assumed that we come into the world with a blueprint that could never be changed. For decades we have been told that every aspect of our life was programmed into our cells at birth and there was nothing we could do to change that. However, the originators of such theories did not understand man or his intrinsic make-up. Neither did they speak from scientific fact. The ability to change is part of what makes us unique in all of creation. We are the only species that has the capacity to change the quality of our life by our choices! This means that everything we learn gives us new choices!

Everything we learn gives us new choices!

With the emergence of cutting-edge biology we now understand that from conception to the grave we are reprogramming our cells, our beliefs and our life map! We are constantly becoming something new or reaffirming that which is! Either way, life is a constant series of choices to transform or to remain the same. But this incredible power to mold our life is our own! We will inevitably default to believe what our culture (tradition) has delivered to us or we will discover the unlimited possibilities of believing God's wonderful plan for man!

Even in the womb we are learning, adapting and changing our basic life blueprint. It is thought that the first "life programming" after conception is primarily the result of the emotional environment experienced by the mother. Many experiments clearly prove that the baby experiences everything the mother experiences. If the mother experiences fear, lack or insecurity as a result of her environment, then the same emotions are experienced by the baby, thereby altering the original programming at conception.

Then at birth there is an entirely new learning process. It seems that the first emotional experience of birth is fear. There is every reason to believe that the sin nature is not, in fact, the inherent desire to do evil, but an inherent tendency toward fear. Fear undermines our trust for the unconditional love of God. If we don't trust God, then we search for alternative ways to be what He says we are. We search for alternate ways to do what He shows us how to do. It is the search for the alternate path that leads to destructive disobedience.

THE TENDENCY TOWARD FEAR

Our modern definition of the word *sin* is itself a learned tradition that plays into our negative concepts of God and life. The Greek word for sin *harmartia* means to miss the mark or not share in the prize.[4] We place the emphasis of missing the mark on how bad we have done. It seems, instead, that the mark we miss is the mark of how great it can be, the prize we have in Him. Sin isn't how bad we are. Sin is how we fail to be who and what we could be in Christ! It's more like the failure to live up to our potential. And all of this is due to our tendency toward fear!

This tendency toward fear causes us to interpret the world around us in a very skewed manner. The result is negative programming. Everything we experience is interpreted in a negative light, which leads to a lifetime of negative beliefs. Add to that the centuries of negative tradition passed down and we become programmed for pessimism, negativity and failure!

Up until about 12 years of age the human mind is perpetually in one of the three deep meditative states delta, theta and alpha. As a result, our interpretation of the world around us is written very deeply in our heart, forming our life beliefs. This explains why some experts say we have developed our life paradigm by the time we are five years old. But we are not choosing these beliefs based on intellectual or even spiritual knowledge. We are choosing these beliefs based on the way the world makes us feel.

The very poignant reality is we are really creating a view of the world by all the things we experience…we are creating a view or interpretation of ourselves! Our view of the world is an extended interpretation of how we see ourselves. This learned interpretation of ourselves doesn't result in a mere intellectual understanding of the world. It becomes a biological blueprint that shapes our health and energy in a way that resists any other interpretation of life. Our body and mind resist changes that would defy our life view!

It is not enough that we grow up having success modeled to us. We need to have success modeled in a way that shows us how it can be easy. Even more to the point, we need to believe something about ourselves that makes us feel that we have the right to succeed. For most that will never happen!

Our view of the world is an extended interpretation of how we see ourselves.

We didn't choose our life lessons and we didn't choose those who would forge our earliest sense of self. But we can choose a new view of life. We can accept God's view of us. We can begin a transformation process that will mold and shape our sense of self and our view of the world around us. Success can become our new norm. We learned to be where we are; we can learn something else! But it all starts with a choice!

Just as we redefined our life blueprint in the womb, we can redefine our life blueprint today. We can learn new information and acquire new tools wherewith we will create new feelings that will become new beliefs. Those beliefs will establish us in a world of success just as surely as our former beliefs established us in the life we now know! How it is isn't how it has to be; it is simply how it is right now! Your possibilities are as limitless as your dreams. The same process that brought you to your current level of success will take you anywhere you choose to go!

CHAPTER 7

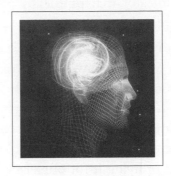

COPING WITH FAILURE

Life is to be lived, not explained.

I N A WORLD DESIGNED to be lived, the "intellectual only," who actually is afraid and distrustful of his feelings, has turned reality upside down. The "intellectual only" is threatened by feelings. They represent the possibility of being out of control. Such people fear the thought of their emotions taking control and causing them to do what their intellectual minds do not condone, thereby damaging their intellectually, ego-driven life!

This is not an attack against an intellectual mind. However, we are not designed to live out of our mind. The mind should help us find functional ways to apply our heart leadings in this natural world. Instead we use the mind to override the heart leadings that do not fit into our programmed paradigm. For man to ever live "as he should,"[1] the heart and mind must function in their God-created priority. The heart must lead; the mind must follow.

We are designed to live out of our heart. Our heart is not the source of irrational emotions that cause us to do stupid things. Our heart is the source of intuitive knowledge that supports who we are and how the world should work! Our heart is the place where we can experience the voice of

God that will always lead us to the most successful outcome. Our heart is the signaling communicator that physically programs the body to be capable of fulfilling its intentions.

We are designed to live out of our heart.

As a result of what I call "intellectual only" people gaining control of the world, everything we know is simply the manifestation of intellectual control. Our schools almost exclusively teach information only. They don't teach us how to do (apply) much of anything. Television and computer games have led us to become a voyeuristic society. We watch others imitate life instead of living it for ourselves. The most predominant therapies for dealing with emotional pain are cognitive therapies that deal more with information than feelings. All of these approaches to life are intellectually driven and at best teach us to cope with a world that is not really fulfilling our deepest needs.

COPING IS MANAGING

In the groundbreaking book *The Healing Code*, Doctors Alex Loyd and Ben Johnson point out that talking about problems over and over not only fails to work, but actually makes problems worse.[2] Most cognitive therapies seek to create an intellectual explanation for the problem and then create from that understanding some coping mechanisms to *manage* the problem. In fact, even the majority of what we learn in church is simply behavior modification mixed with coping mechanisms that are given spiritual terminology. The world isn't getting better. It's getting worse, and we're learning to cope with it, accept it and manage how we react about it.

Coping may help us manage a problem, but it does not deal with the root of the problem. In fact, coping can become a form of intellectual denial. If we get really good at coping, then we tend to get really bad at noticing. The problem doesn't go away; we simply stop noticing it. But it is still there. As one book title so aptly puts it, feelings buried alive never die! Coping facilitates our daily rotting from the inside out while not noticing it or doing anything about the beliefs that create the problem!

Loyd and Johnson go on to refer to Dr. John Sarno, professor at New York University Medical School. His research confirms that adult chronic

Coping does not deal with the root of the problem.

pain and chronic health problems result from the suppression of destructive cellular memories.[3] Coping is a form of suppression. Suppression is like putting your problems in a pressure cooker. You may not be able to see them, but the pressure is building and eventually will erupt in some destructive manner. Learning to live with failure is a form of suppression, or coping. You may be able to give an intellectual reason for why it is how it is, but that does not do anything about how it is. And furthermore it does nothing to reduce the internal stress that is mounting and multiplying your inability to succeed.

Failure and lack are so contrary to the way we were wired that they tend to lead to deep feelings of guilt and shame. Guilt and shame are incredibly destructive emotions that become self-fulfilling prophecies. Guilt comes from the feeling that we have done something wrong. When people are not able to satisfy their inherent need for success it tends to lead to the negative introspection that insists, "I must have done something wrong; otherwise, my life would be better." Guilt is a pathway that leads to shame!

Shame, on the other hand, goes beyond the feelings that I have done something wrong to the feelings that "something is wrong with me." Shame is the rejection of self! According to some research shame is the most destructive of all negative internal responses. To reject self is to enter into a conspiracy of self-destruction with the world and all that is in it! If I am "wrong or bad," then I must reject me and I must be punished.

Condemnation is the usual result of guilt and shame. Condemnation is the inner feeling that since I feel this way about myself I should be punished. That self-induced punishment can come in the form of sickness, destructive relationships, failed business or any form of self-destructive behavior…as such, unsuccessful! A heart that is overrun with condemnation will never believe for success because it doesn't feel worthy of success!

COPING IS NOT CURING

There are many socially acceptable coping mechanisms that are passed off as therapy. There are even more coping mechanisms that are less socially acceptable. Drugs, alcohol, sex and any other addictive vice is a common coping mechanism. Sadly, we are led to believe that stopping the behavior and managing through meetings and other therapies is a cure. While I am a strong supporter of support groups and even coping skills, apart from being combined with heart beliefs, they exacerbate the problems. The truth is the cure is correcting the thing that makes us need to cope. If we are living a positive, enjoyable life harmonious with a healthy sense of self, then we don't have negative emotions with which to cope!

When we find ourselves in the throes of failure of any kind the most common coping mechanism is blame. We must find or create a suitable nemesis on which to blame our failure. If we cannot find an individual to blame, then we will blame the world in general. One of the ways to realize we are still simply coping is our tendency to complain and criticize. Complaining, which actually creates more internal stress, is a clear signal that we still need excuses for the conditions of our life that our heart simply will not accept!

The cure is correcting the thing that makes us need to cope.

People who are not living as they are "wired" struggle to find contentment. Learning to cope is taking an antacid. The problem doesn't go away, you don't feel just right, but your symptoms don't appear to be bad enough to consider yourself sick. Yet all the while your body is preparing for disease. Coping drains us of physical and emotional energy and masks the symptoms but never solves the real problem.

With the emergent discovery of cellular memories science has opened a door wider than they can ever close. If there is the possibility of cellular programming that involves past generations, then this means there is cellular memory and programming that goes all the way back to creation. We were created in the likeness and image of God! Man was, in fact, the only being that was not created by the spoken word. God actually created us by breathing some of who He is into the bodies He created for us. We are made from who God is! He is in our DNA. We are wired to be like God.

Despite all our destructive tendencies, regardless of the fall in the garden, taking into account generations of perversion and corruption, man still has in him, at the core of his being, some Divine sense that must be satisfied in a life of meaning and success. When we accept (coping is a form of accepting) a life of failure there is an internal conflict in our genes. The cellular memory of who we are supposed to be versus who we have been programmed to accept is in conflict. It will create stress and internal conflict. The thing we must remember is programming can be changed, but how we are wired will never change. By dealing with the heart, we can reprogram ourselves to function more consistently with how we were created.

God is in our DNA. We are wired to be like God.

Internal Life Resources has developed a heart transformation program called Heart Physics®. Heart Physics® is based on more than 30 years of research and clinical application. Heart Physics® employs the internal tools built in you from creation to influence your heart and create a sense of self that knows how to do nothing but succeed! By changing your sense of self, failure becomes intolerable. Coping is unacceptable. Instead of coping transformation becomes the process for dealing the life that you did not choose!

Instead of learning to cope and instead of simply changing our behavior, through Heart Physics® we can get to the heart of the issues: what we believe in our heart. When people come to me to help them solve their problems they usually ask, "What do I need to *do*?" They are always surprised when I respond, "It doesn't matter what you do. Nothing will change until you identify what you *believe* in your heart. You don't need to know what to do. You need to know what to believe…in your heart!"

To live a life of success without all the destructive stress factors, you have to start with your beliefs. In our Heart Physics® program, "Creating Wealth," we give you the tools to address your heart beliefs. But keep reading. You'll learn a lot more about your heart beliefs and how to reprogram yourself as you turn each page.

CHAPTER 8

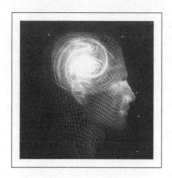

IS SUCCESS SUPPOSED TO BE HARD?

Success is as hard as we make it. But in the final analysis success is never as painful or as difficult as failure!

THERE IS SOMETHING WOVEN deep in the fabric of mankind that draws us to what we believe to be enjoyable and repels us from what we believe to be painful. After all, we were designed to live in paradise. We were never wired for a hard life! Therefore, it is inherent for us to pursue pleasure and avoid pain!

Even when we deeply desire something, if there is a threat of pain, we may not pursue what we desire. If the imagined pain seems more certain than the possibility of pleasure, then we will find ourselves paralyzed and not understand why. However, if the pleasure is reasonably sure and it outweighs the pain, we will wade through mountains of pain and difficulty with an unwavering persistence to reach our goals.

For most people, the idea of success and prosperity is choked with the illusion of pain and hardship. For many the pain seems sure, while success seems to be only a remote possibility! On our internal scale of pain and pleasure our beliefs calculate the imagined probabilities and take us on a course we may have never consciously chosen. But how did we get those beliefs? Who calibrated our internal scales? Simple! Everything we have ever seen, heard and tried created a system of beliefs concerning success that subconsciously guides our course!

Every poor man will tell you, "Success is difficult!" But is a poor man qualified to advise you concerning success? Every person who has failed to live his or her dream can expound on the hardships of realizing one's dream. But is that person really qualified to advise you on the tenets of living your dream? Those who have learned to live a hard life will tell you how hard life should be…based on their experience. Far too often we are influenced by those who have never made the journey we pursue! One of the oldest tenets of wisdom is to only seek counsel from those knowledgeable and successful in the field of our endeavors!

WHAT DID YOU SEE MODELED?

In the book *Rich Dad Poor Dad*, author Robert Kiyosaki presents the general concept that for those who were raised in families where prosperity was modeled it was easy for the successive generations. But most of the world has not seen the model of success. If they have seen success, there are few who have seen it made easy. Even those who have seen financial success usually have seen it exact a devastating toll on families and personal health.

There is a familiar adage that says, "If you want to make a million dollars, find someone who has and do what they did." Maybe we're asking the wrong people! If we want to find success without great difficulty and personal devastation, then maybe we need to find a new model. Based on this "barefoot wisdom," by asking the wrong people about success I may, in fact, be contributing to my already flawed thinking! I may be making it harder just by asking the wrong people! What if I could find someone who has succeeded and he or she knew how to do it easily? I could learn something that could change my entire success paradigm!

The man commonly acknowledged to be the wisest and richest man to ever live gives quite a different point of view concerning success than is commonly embraced. *"…The race is not to the swift, nor the battle to the strong, nor bread to the wise, nor riches to men of understanding, nor favor to men of skill; but time and chance happen to them all."*[1] In other words, opportunity comes to all men! It seems that the wisest, richest man to ever live brings all of the success factors into perspective. It is not about how hard you work, it is not about how smart you are, it is not about all of the things that make it hard. Success is about the capacity to see and seize opportunity when it comes!

Success is about the capacity to see and seize opportunity when it comes!

Time and chance happen to everyone; the question is, do you have the heart (the beliefs) to recognize and act accordingly when opportunity comes your way? Beliefs are filters; because of what they allow you to see, they shape your perception. How you see and interpret the world around you is some mixture of reality and personal beliefs. Beliefs not only alter how you see the world, they also alter how you interact with the world. Before you can make an intellectual decision about the opportunities that surround you, your personal beliefs will alter your perception and your responses!

Henry Ford coined the phrase, "Whether you think you can or can't, you're probably right!" The mind always seeks equilibrium. It validates its thoughts by shaping perception and thereby creating the illusion of circumstances that prove its perception. If you think success is hard, then you will make it hard to succeed as a way to validate your opinion. If you think prosperity will cost you your family, then it probably will. Whatever you think about success you will find a way to produce. In other words, it will be as hard and costly as you think it to be!

The one thing we must accept is that our every idea about nearly every aspect of life was learned. It was either learned *from* someone or by our own trial and error. There is no reason to believe that "someone" knew what he or she was talking about. Likewise, unless we learned how to succeed without difficulty, there is no reason to believe our past experience to be the definitive model of success! We know what we have experienced. Unfortunately, our experience is far too often the validation of our flawed beliefs. It is seldom a reflection of reality!

A BETTER WAY TO PROSPER

The writer of Proverbs said, *"The blessing of the Lord makes one rich, and He adds no sorrow with it."*[2] That word for sorrow, according to *Strong's Concordance*, is toil or grievous labor.[3] To put it in layman's terminology, "God has a way to prosper that isn't hard and painful!" If the way we were taught to prosper was difficult…there is a better way!

At one point I realized that something in me was resistant to success in a specific area of my life. In other areas I was quite comfortable succeeding and prospering. But in one key area I would excel to a point and then hit what seemed like an invisible barrier. Based on Proverbs 4:23, I knew the problem was not external but internal. It was a limiting belief that created an imaginary external boundary! *"Keep* [guard] *your heart with all diligence, for out of it spring the issues of life."* The word *issues* could just as well have been translated as "boundaries."

The boundaries in my life are not the result of some external resistance. The boundaries in my life, and in this particular case in an area of my personal success, was the product of my personal beliefs. With a little heart work I discovered that I held to a belief that said, "In this area I could not keep my family and experience success." The two seemed mutually exclusive! The reason for this belief is what I had seen. My beliefs were the product of observations. I had observed those whose families were the price of their success! But there was a better way. There is always a better way!

There is always a better way!

You see, I don't want to find someone who made a million dollars and do what he did. I want to find someone who made a million dollars, enjoyed life, lived his dream *and* maintained great relationships. I don't want to simply do what he did; I want to know what he believed!

So if you repeatedly encounter that immovable impasse that holds you captive to a certain level of success, then you can be assured it is nothing more than a belief. The great thing about beliefs is that they can be changed! That change starts with a choice. Now you know success is *not* supposed to be hard. You may have thought you are not smart enough or not strong enough. No matter what you think your limitations to be, this is nothing but a belief that says, "This is too hard!" Hold on for the ride of your life. You are equipping yourself to go where you've never been, to tear down limiting boundaries and to create a new paradigm!

CHAPTER 9

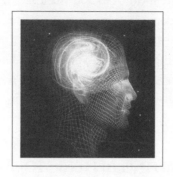

LEARNING TO SUCCEED

We live in the illusion of what we have learned. We can learn something different!

To BORROW AN EARLIER quote by Tony Robbins and dozens of other life coaches and teachers, *practice doesn't make perfect, it only makes permanent!* Living within our current limitations has been perfected by the repeated use of wrong thoughts, inferior skills and self-defeating decisions. Because we were led by our mind we kept pulling out the same tools in every situation—only to be surprised by the same outcome.

Just as surely as practicing the *wrong* thing over and over teaches us to do something wrong, practicing the *same* things over and over teach us to do things the same. We may get better at what we know but we don't actually improve our overall skills or expand our boundaries. It would be like a golfer who is good off the tee but weak on the green. It would be a waste of time to go to the driving range and hit endless buckets of balls. He's got that part of the game conquered. He's got to get on the green if he's going to change his game!

Everything about the mind and body says, "Get out of the rut; do something different." If you do physical exercise, then you know constant growth demands that you change your routine. Otherwise your body adapts and falls into stagnation. Progress slows to a near halt! If you desire to keep your mind sharp, then you have to learn new things. People who keep learning stay sharp and focused well into old age! Everything about the way you are wired demands that you be ever growing and ever expanding.

MY LIMITING BELIEFS STOPPED ME

When I first entered the world of sales and marketing I worked for a company that sold financial products and services. I could do an incredible presentation. I was very persuasive. I was good at reading people and understanding what types of questions they wanted answered, but I was terrible at making phone calls. When you're in sales the first actual step toward making a sale is making a contact! If you don't make the contact you don't get in front of the people. If you don't get in front of the people it doesn't matter how good you do anything else, you're not going to make the sale.

Until it was brought to my attention by my mentor, I did not realize I was creating busy work as a way to avoid productive work. Why? The productive work was something I didn't like to do. The busy work was something I enjoyed, plus it gave me the deceitful feeling that I was actually trying. I wasn't trying something wrong; I was just repeating something familiar so I could feel productive. Every day that I did it I got better at it, but it never made my sales go up. Eventually I gritted my teeth, faced the fear and forced myself to do what I hated. In less than a year I hit a record-breaking point and just when I should have been really coming into the money I quit and took a job making a fraction of what I would have made if I had stayed with the company.

Why did I quit? I had learned to succeed the hard way…and it was hard! Something I have learned about us humans is that we will not continue to do what creates too much discomfort for very long. The money I made on my sales was not reasonable compensation for the degree of discomfort I faced every time I picked up the telephone.

In subsequent businesses I faced the same dread. I found ways to make money…but, boy, was it hard! So I read books about making calls. I developed systems that made it somewhat easier, but in the end it was still intellectual ideas mixed with a lot of will power. When there is a struggle between feelings and willpower, in the end feelings will always eventually win!

When the systems and books didn't do it for me, I tried a subliminal program for overcoming procrastination. After about a week of using this tool, I would find myself waking up at 4 a.m. ready to work. I didn't procrastinate! But when it came to making contact calls I was still miserable.

When there is a struggle between feelings and willpower, in the end feelings will always eventually win!

What I thought was a procrastination problem was a belief problem. It was not just my belief about making contact calls; it was actually my belief about success. I had some limiting beliefs about success. Contact calls were simply the place where the limiting belief was able to stop me.

Limiting beliefs are sort of like diseases in the body. If you eat foods that cause inflammation, then it may have some systemic effect throughout the body. But the place the eating pattern will cause you the most harm is in the part of your body that is the weakest. As that inflammation grows the part of your body that is the weakest link is the part that becomes diseased first.

If you go to a typical doctor, the underlying cause may never be diagnosed or discussed. He will simply look at the organ that is diseased, remove the organ or treat it with some kind of medication. That medication is like external motivation or intellectual stimuli. It brings just enough relief to think it's working, but in time something else will go wrong. Likewise, no matter what skills you learn, what books you read or what motivation you receive, it will only be a momentary relief and then the underlying cause—the belief—emerges again!

By identifying your limiting belief and installing a new empowering belief you instruct your heart. Learning to be a success is a heart change that renews the way you see yourself and the way you see your destiny. It's not a temporary fix. It doesn't address the symptom. It goes to the core of the problem! My issue involving contact calls was a symptom of my need to fail. It was the weakest link in the emotional chain. Did I have issues about calling? Yes! But the fear of calling was not the real issue; it was a symptom. I removed the cause and then I found a way to deal with the symptom. By removing your underlying cause you will no longer move forward only to fall backward. Your inherently weak spot is no longer vulnerable to the pathology of failure! You have removed the "inflammation" and now learning new skills and systems will actually benefit.

LET YOUR HEART LEAD

When the mind leads we learn information in the hopes that the information will lead to wisdom, or in other words, practical application. When the heart leads we walk the path of wisdom to a greater success. With the mind we learn scads of details in the hope that something will "stick" and take us over the tipping point. But when the heart leads it takes us to the specific skills we need to learn, the specific avenues to explore and the perfect contacts for the next step. Plus, when the heart leads, we permanently break through the limiting emotions that previously exploited our most basic weakness and brought about the demise of our dreams!

Recently I realized I had reached a financial impasse. I was topped out in my current ability to expand my goals. Expanding my goals necessitated the creation of more funds, which was not intimidating. I knew I could expand my heart to create more finances. But there were other things I needed that I did not know where to look for or how to find. If I had allowed my mind to lead I would have assessed all the factors and made financial projections while simultaneously trying to make connections with people who had the skill set to help me accomplish my goals. One of my great frustrations was the fact that I had hired a number of talented people who were supposed to be able to do the technical things I needed done. After hundreds of thousands of wasted dollars I was still stuck. I was out of resources. My mind did not know where to look!

I began to do the Painting a New Life Picture exercise, part of the Creating Wealth Heart Physics® Program. Fifty-seven days into the exercise, I reached a place of complete peace and stopped doing the exercise. Within a few days of reaching the place of peace, I met some people who had the technical skills I needed. Within 21 days my income increased 57 percent. Then I negotiated the financing on a piece of property I had for sale that would put nearly one million dollars in my hands. None of those things happened through an orchestrated, planned effort. They were circumstances around me that had to conform to the beliefs of my heart.

In my early 30s I began studying martial arts. It was great exercise! I knew I needed something that was fun and organized, or I would never stick to it. I looked at many forms of what are called external arts. They have a lot of emphasis on memorizing a lot of maneuvers and then employing them with great strength. Although they were great for some people, it just didn't feel right for me. Eventually I found the right fit. It was an internal art that had more to do with being sensitive and responsive than it did with memorizing and executing all the right moves.

When I reached the stage of competing I asked my teacher for advice. In typical oriental fashion he gave an answer that sounded like something Mr. Miyage would have said to the Karate Kid. "What should I do?" I asked. In true ancient wisdom he replied, "Forget everything you know." Fortunately the competition I was entering was very scaled down. There was no real risk of getting hurt.

Afterward when we met at my house to practice I asked what he meant. He said, "The mind only gets in the way. If you try to compete with your mind it is too slow. Everything will depend on how fast you can think, process and respond." Then he continued, "You have practiced; you know all the moves. Now just step into the competition and trust what you know. What you need will come to you! When your opponent strikes you will not be there. You will move before he can successfully attack. Don't try to remember what you know, just trust your instincts." That day I learned a secret that I could take into every aspect of my life. I don't have to intellectually figure it all out; I simply need to trust what is in me.

Several years ago I learned Photo Reading. Because I am constantly learning and researching I needed a way to intake massive quantities of information and recall it pretty much on demand. I found this through Photo Reading. In Photo Reading I basically read two pages per second, about 25,000 words per minute, with a comprehension of about 80 percent.

> *I don't have to intellectually figure it all out; I simply need to trust what is in me.*

My two greatest challenges of Photo Reading were these: Learning a new way to learn, and learning a new way to know! In school we were taught to hard focus. We see one word at a time and focus on that word. We read linearly across the page one word at a time.

Science tells us that when you hard focus, as you and I were taught in school, the number of nerves activated in your eyes greatly decreases, which means you cannot take in as much information. By doing what's called a soft focus and never looking directly at the page, you activate many more nerves and allow yourself to take in much more information. As you flip the pages at approximately one page turn per second, which exposes you to two pages per second, you constantly affirm, "See the page, read the page, this is entering my other-than-conscious mind," and other similar affirmations.

It was so hard to trust that I was getting any of it. You see, when you finished you couldn't recall one thing about what you had read. You had to allow your mind to process the information and let it seep into your conscious mind. Then the really hard part is when you want to recall the information.

When I was getting my certification as a substance abuse counselor for the State of Alabama, I Photo Read the entire training program in about 7 minutes and reviewed it for about 40 minutes. That's it! When I went in to take my exam, I looked down at the quiz and realized that I consciously knew the answers to very few of the questions. I almost panicked! In order to qualify to open a clinic I had to pass this test.

After a moment of "sweating bullets" I closed my eyes, went to my Heart Zone[1] and affirmed, "All of this information is in my other-than-conscious mind; it is available for my use when I need it, desire it or request it. I will open my eyes and answer these questions accurately because I now request the information that I need to come into my conscious mind." The next step in the process was completely different and more challenging than almost anything I've ever done. The answers were not in my mind in the form of specific words. I only had a gentle intuitive sense about the answer to each question. Intellectually I had no idea if they were the right answers, but I followed my inner man.

More than anything else, learning to succeed is about learning to believe!

I made such a high score on the test that the instructor thought I should have taken the next level of certification. The score, however, was the least important thing that happened for me that day. You see, I took my teacher's advice, "Step into the situation and forget all you know and allow what you need to come to you." Learning to succeed from a heart perspective doesn't mean you don't learn skills. It by no means devalues academic learning. But it does mean that when your heart beliefs support being a success, you won't need to mentally strive for all the right answers. You stay in the place of peace, forget everything you know and allow what you need to know at that moment to come forth. More than anything else, learning to succeed is about learning to believe!

What I have learned will come to me when I need it, if my beliefs support my success. But there is an even greater aspect of learning to succeed! God speaks to your heart. He is the Creator of all things. He knows the answers to all things. He knows how to accomplish all things. He will breathe into your heart things that are beyond all you have ever seen, thought or imagined. Learning to succeed is about learning to trust that still small voice that will lead you into your greatest dream!

Learning to succeed beyond your present academic knowledge or current skill set is about learning to listen to and follow your heart. It means learning to trust the voice of your heart instead of the ranting of your mind. It will mean making as great of an investment into your heart as you have made into your mind! It is about learning to walk a new path…the way of the heart! Just like learning to trust the Photo Reading process I have to learn to trust the way of the heart. By using Heart Physics® tools, you will have the opportunity to implement proven, trusted methods of developing your heart. In time, you will trust your heart more than you trust anything else. It will be the first place you look for the wisdom to succeed. It will be the first place you go to find all of life's solutions. The way of the heart is a way of peace that passes anything you have every experienced with your mind!

CHAPTER 10

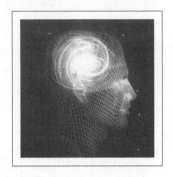

A JOURNEY INTO THE UNKNOWN

*The truth with the most potential to set free always has
the most potential to offend!*

WHY WOULD THE TRUTH that has the greatest capacity to change our life for the good be the truth to which we are most resistant? Simple! It threatens our deepest vulnerabilities! Of the many things that could make us resistant, possibly the two to which we are most resistant are first, that which touches our self-worth, and second, that which takes us into the unknown. Every aspect of our life, every decision, is a product of our sense of self. We will dedicate an entire chapter to this issue, but for now we must address our issue with the "unknown."

There are many levels of filters through which we view the world and through which we interpret input. One filter through which all data is processed is that of pain and pleasure. On a certain level every decision we make is related to our perception or anticipation of pain or pleasure. If we perceive the threat of pain, then we will withdraw from a situation. If we perceive enough pleasure, then we will pursue a situation. Perceived pain and pleasure is always a key factor to conscious and subconscious decision-making. It is important that the key word here is *perceived*. It really isn't about how much pain and pleasure really exists; it is about our perception of pain and pleasure! Faulty beliefs play a major role in disrupting our capacity to properly evaluate pain and pleasure.

There is much debate about which force is the most powerful—the anticipation of pain or the expectation of pleasure. Personally, I think that is a variable based on behavior patterns and life experience. But as often as not, if there is the possibility of enough pleasure and the pain is not absolute, then we will run the risk. This happens when we do something dishonest for the temporary gain, not really considering the possibility of imprisonment. On the other hand, if the potential for pain is greater than the potential for pleasure, then we will withdraw. This could occur when you are offered a job promotion but your fear of learning new skills causes you to refuse the offer. Pain and pleasure are part of our basic survival mechanism.

WIRED FOR PLEASURE

The reason for the pain and pleasure factor stems from the way we were wired. We were wired for success and happiness—or pleasure. Just think about it. Man lived in a garden where every need was met. At the time the atmosphere of the Earth was different. The temperature and all the environmental factors were proportioned in such a way as to produce the ideal living conditions! Man knew nothing but fulfillment, success, peace and happiness.

Even our nervous system points out that we are wired for success. The autonomic nervous system has two distinct functions: thrive or survive. The parasympathetic nervous system carries on all the necessary functions to keep us healthy, strong and energetic—thriving. We don't even have to think about it. It just happens because we are wired for it.

On the other hand, the sympathetic nervous system kicks in when there is a perceived threat—survive! The moment anything occurs within our range of awareness that is perceived as a threat the bodily functions stop the nurturing process. Immediately hundreds of known bodily functions change. Different hormones are released, digestion stops, blood flow goes to the limbs, respiration changes and even more. All this occurs without conscious thought. It happens as a means to deliver us from the threat, or more appropriately the perceived threat: survival!

It is essential that we establish the awareness that a perceived threat is just as powerful at influencing change in the body as a real threat. In a real threat there is physical action that occurs that diminishes the flood of adrenaline and other hormones designed to motivate to action; you run or fight! The body uses all of these hormones; the threat is removed and the body can return to thriving: pleasure. But when the threat is only perceived, when it comes from worrying and rehearsing your fears, there is no way for these "natural stimulants" to be utilized. So they stay in the body wreaking physiological and emotional imbalance, both of which alter our perception and ability to function!

The problem is the unknown. To succeed beyond what I've had in the past is to venture into the unknown. The "unknown" is perceived as a threat. Therefore it produces fear and the possibility of pain or displeasure. When faced with an unknown the majority of people begin, with no awareness or conscious effort, to make a physiological shift from their parasympathetic to their sympathetic nervous system. All of the same changes take place that prepare us for a physical threat. Some people get a queasy feeling in their gut or begin to feel nervous. They take that as a sign not to venture forward. They fail to realize that instead of an intuitive heart warning, the fear is triggering their bodily function. They feel anxious, nervous and unsure; they associate this with a signal to halt!

> *The "unknown" is perceived as a threat. Therefore it produces fear and the possibility of pain or displeasure.*

Throughout your entire life, these same feelings came in times of threat. Maybe as a child a dog bit you, you were bullied by older children or you experienced any thousands of negative threatening situations that proved to you, "When I feel this, something bad is about to happen!" This is called an association. Your brain associates this feeling with painful experiences. This "feeling" is then believed to be a warning of danger. This means you will either stop moving forward or run when you have this "feeling." These associations are responsible for the majority of people's decisions even before they have the opportunity to rationally think them through!

Every experience since conception has been recorded in our cells and can be instantly recalled. When faced with any new challenge, before we have opportunity to think it through, on a subconscious level the current opportunity is evaluated in light of all of our past failures and successes and everything we have ever seen and done. In a nanosecond the idea is rejected or accepted based on many factors, the least of which is unfamiliarity! The issue is what is not familiar is *perceived* as a threat!

The problem is this. If I am facing the opportunity to make more money than I have ever made, that is an unknown. If it is something that will cause me to face too much change, then it is an unknown. In fact, succeeding at anything beyond my current level of success is an unknown, which means it will produce a degree of fear. Based on our perception of pain and pleasure we instantly fight against or run from the very opportunity for which we have been working, praying and planning our entire life!

THE UNDERLYING ISSUE

Although there are numerous psychological factors involved in this, there is an underlying heart issue that must be brought into the forefront of our life plan for success. When the potential for success exceeds our sense of self it will cause fear, stress and withdrawal. Sometimes the withdrawal is when we shoot down the opportunity up front. Or even more painful is when we push ourselves to risk it "this time." When our success grows very far beyond our sense of self, we will subconsciously find some way to destroy the opportunity. This is the basis for many self-destructive patterns.

As you will see in Chapter 13, until you expand your sense of self (self-worth), success beyond your current level will end in incredible levels of stress and/or destruction. A person who stubbornly persists in living beyond his or her comfort zone usually self-destructs. It doesn't end with the loss of an opportunity; it ends with the loss of health and possibly life!

The heart is where our sense of self is "housed." Researchers really don't know where the physical heart and the spiritual heart overlap, but there is no separating the two. So when I speak of the heart I am speaking of an internal function that is the root of all your emotions and beliefs. It is the root of who you are and how you see yourself! As such, as I described before, the heart is like a thermostat. Your self-worth is the setting. Like any thermostat, it may allow you to do things a little beneath who you believe yourself to be or it may allow you to rise slightly above your sense of self. But in the end, it will cause the heat pump to kick in and bring the temperature (sense of self) back to the setting. Any attempt to abide beyond your sense of self for a prolonged period of time causes the furnace (or air conditioning) to run constantly, creating excessive use of energy and creating stress.

Only a change in heart will allow you to safely venture beyond your current thermostat setting. By dealing with your heart you will reset the thermostat. There will be no additional stress or wasteful expenditures of energy. Heart Physics® is designed to give you the tools you need to expand your life to limitless boundaries by expanding your sense of self. When you have a healthy self-worth, the way you think about and process "unknowns" is completely different.

When you have a healthy self-worth, the way you think about and process "unknowns" is completely different.

In the book *Transforming Stress*, Doc Childre and Deborah Rozman, Ph.D. point out that stress is not a fixed phenomenon. What creates stress in one individual may be exhilarating to another. They compare it to riding a roller coaster. Some people are in the front throwing their hands in the air laughing and screaming for joy. Others are in the back covering their eyes and screaming for fear. They are all on the same ride. What's the difference? Perception![1]

When you alter your sense of self your every perception is changed. That which used to threaten you is now overlooked. That which once made you cower in fear is now an exciting challenge. How you see yourself moves you from the back of the roller coaster hiding in fear to the front of the roller coaster enjoying the ride of your life!

As you incorporate new Heart Resources into your life you will be able to turn the stress of the unknown into the excitement of an adventure. When the fear is gone you can open your eyes and see the world of opportunity that is waiting for you to take the journey!

CHAPTER 11

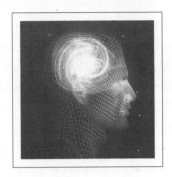

RULES FOR TRANSFORMATION

*Change is the only natural constant in life; it is the only key to a
better tomorrow!*

THE GREATEST ONGOING STRUGGLE of every human being is the
conflict between the thoughts of the mind and the beliefs of the
heart. Because of complete unawareness of the heart, few people
have any comprehension of the source of this struggle—and so they have
no cure. Thoughts emerge from two different sources: the mind and the
heart. The thoughts of the mind are academic, intellectual. They are based
on that which is learned or perceived by the five senses. The thoughts of
the heart are intuitive and based primarily on the beliefs that create our
sense of self. One has to do with information about the world around us.
The other has to do with internal awareness. Much of the internal awareness is the programming derived from how we interpret that information.

Beliefs of the heart are realized by our abiding feelings. They are
actualized by subconsciously guiding our decisions to keep our behavior
consistent with who we believe (feel) ourselves to be! The ongoing internal
conflict for all individuals is the conflict between who they believe they are
in their heart and who they think they should be in their minds. Who we

79

think we should be in our minds is usually a matter of what we think our behavior should be. This manifests when we desire to act or function one way and do something very different.

When you are young you develop your sense of self. If your sense of self is tied to lack or difficulty, then that will set your "thermostat." But as you grow, as you read books about life, love and success, or as you attend motivational seminars and church services, you may put forth great effort toward positive thinking. But you find that regardless of all the training, success is seemingly impossible. This could mean success in any area, in finances, relationships or health. This scenario is the most common situation that I see in helping develop others for success. They think the information they have stored in their mind is powerful enough to change their life. It isn't! But it *is* powerful enough to create internal conflict between their heart and mind!

> *The ongoing internal conflict for all individuals is the conflict between who they believe they are in their heart and who they think they should be in their minds.*

At this point the people who are serious about change theorize all the reasons they are not changing, which are usually little more than self-judgment. Then they theorize how they will bring about the change. This is usually some process that is little more than behavior modification and willpower. They will try, only to fail again because they are ignorant of or refuse to play by the rules...that is, the rules of the heart. It does not matter how sincere you may be. The heart is not influenced by your sincerity, your knowledge or your intelligence. Rather, your heart functions from some very simple rules that are designed for your protection!

YOU'VE GOT TO PLAY BY THE RULES

The thoughts of the mind have the ability to influence your emotions. But emotions are short-term. Emotions are based on your last thoughts. Where you focus your attention creates emotions based on what you're thinking. Like follows like! Those emotions will abide momentarily. But as your focus shifts from your last thoughts, your emotions change to match your new thoughts. If, however, your attention is not focused you will default to the beliefs (thoughts and feelings) of the heart—that is, how you really feel about you.

"As a man thinks in his heart, so is he."[1] You will habitually act, think and feel in accordance to the thoughts and feelings of your heart. You can't escape the thoughts and feelings of the heart by positive thinking because no one can stay selectively focused for a very long period of time. When you stop putting forth effort your feelings will revert back to your default…your sense of self. You live out of your sense of self, like it or not! So after attempting a new plan, attending a new seminar or mustering the strength for one more try, the majority of people default back to their abiding sense of self. The temporary change is nothing more than momentary intellectual motivation, a little inspiration and willpower.

You live out of your sense of self, like it or not!

Don't immediately assume the seminar or training to be a loss. It can help you manage your life better, and when you change the beliefs of your heart this information which now creates conflict will become a powerful tool for improving your quality of life. But information has never made anyone permanently change apart from his or her heart being influenced.

The beliefs of the heart, or what you believe about you, are the source of your root, long-term, abiding feelings. It is the seat of your overall emotional health. Your sense of self is the filter through which you look at and interpret the world. Whether a situation is an opportunity or a threat is all determined by your sense of self. Change your heart and change your life. The world or anything outside you doesn't need to change for you to experience success. When you change your heart (your sense of self) you will see the world differently. You will see opportunity where you once saw danger. You will have hope where others give up. You will succeed not because of what you do but because you *are* a success in your heart!

When you change your heart you will see the world differently.

By now you've got to be saying, "Great! I'll change my heart…. But how do I do that?" Everyone has changed his or her heart at one time or another, but it was usually by default. It may not even have been something you wanted or tried to do, but you can look back to a time when you know you changed. Unfortunately, when most people look back they identify times they changed for the worse and can't really understand how it happened. Even though they didn't realize it, they changed because they followed the rules of the heart.

ONLY YOU CAN CHANGE YOUR HEART

When we look back at times of change we nearly always focus on and blame some outside source. We can see clearly what someone did to hurt or inflict pain. Since the change happened at that moment, it seems obvious: *You* did this to me! But the truth is no one outside of us has ever changed our heart. Outside influences may have initiated a sequence of events that resulted in a heart change, but it was our internal actions that followed a set of defined rules of the heart that brought about the change. The heart is designed to resist change that we do not choose. We have been wired so that no one can influence our heart except us. Other than what happens at the new birth, all of our heart changes are made by us. God lives in our spirit. He only moves into the realm of our heart when faith is present. Faith follows a very definable path of influencing our heart. Other people do things that influence our five senses, but it is what we do internally with that data that determines if it becomes written on our heart. Heart Physics® will give people the tools they need to write on their heart and so bring about the desired changes at a heart level. It defines the rules of the heart and, in fact, shows us how to use them in exact compliance to how we were wired. We have seen countless people make major life transformations when they learned how to influence their heart.

Your heart resists any attempts at change that are not made the way you were wired! Any endeavor to change that is based solely on information or from the outside is resisted. The heart is trying to protect the beliefs that you already have accepted as your own. But it is also resistant to any process that isn't based on how it was created to function: the rules for transformation!

The heart is designed to resist change that we do not choose.

There are two factors present when heart changes occur: information and emotion. That emotion is most powerful when it is emotion associated with how you feel about you. If you are told you are bad, if you think you are unlovable, then this type of input creates powerful emotional feelings connected to your sense of self! It does the same thing when you have any experience wherein you attach personal significance. Suppose you walk into a room full of people and none of them acknowledge you. You pass a judgment. You assume the reason why no one acknowledged you was, "No one really likes me!" Remember, to assume "why" is to pass judgment. That judgment gives significance to the behavior of others. But your judgment also determines how that behavior will affect you. Nothing affects you beyond the significance you attach to it!

There are times, particularly while children, that a heart belief can be created in one emotional exchange. The reason we are so susceptible when we are young is because we are in a meditative state until about the age of 11 or 12. Our brain waves from about 5 years old to around 11 are in the alpha state. This is the state that people reach while meditating, praying or while in deep relaxation. At this state it is much easier to accept information at a very deep level. This is a formative stage of life that combines intellectual learning coupled with almost direct access to the subconscious.

When information is coupled with strong emotion, particularly emotion that is based on personal perception, it can be written on the heart and become a part of our sense of self. From that moment forward our every decision is affected by that altered view of ourselves! For a child in the alpha state, the intellectual capacity to stop much of the outside data is bypassed.

The most powerful tool, beyond immediate integration, is when we think and rethink about an event. When remembering an event we recreate the same emotions we originally experienced. If, however, we add some new significance, then we create new emotions. That means the rethinking has a new ability to affect our heart. Rethinking things until we create the associated emotions is a form of meditation. Everyone meditates and everyone influences his or her own heart, but it is usually a default mechanism that is used for destruction not self-development. Everyone knows the rules for transformation; people have simply never identified them and used them by choice.

MAKING A DECISION

So many times while we are in these states of strong emotion we reach a conclusion about ourselves and make strong definitive statements. "I will never let that happen to me again." "No one will ever hurt me again." "I will never trust anyone with my money again." This is basically a vow. The Bible warns against making vows. Vows have an incredible power to influence our heart. The word *vow*, according to the *Theological Wordbook of the Old Testament*, is more than just making a promise to do something. It is connected to uttering blessings and curses; it is to bind ourselves to something.[2] When we make a vow, an internal statement in times of deep, strong feelings, we may forever change our lives. We bind ourselves and our identity to the thing we have uttered.

Everyone knows the rules for transformation; people have simply never identified them and used them by choice.

We did not realize at that moment we were making a decision, but we were. In one emotional instant we implemented all the factors required for influencing our heart. We got into a meditative state. The meditative state is when we ponder, consider, rehearse or rethink an issue until we create the associated emotion. Then we personalized it. We saw it affecting us or being about us. Then we chose a new belief to which we deeply and emotionally committed ourselves.

Everyone meditates! Yet some because of unfounded religious ideas or intellectualism deny, decry and state complete disdain for meditation. Many declare as wicked a process that is not only natural, but also the only tool for transformation we have been given. That which God has given for our good we ignorantly reject as evil, leaving ourselves totally helpless against the effects of life. Regardless of what such people think, they not only meditate, but that meditation shaped their life. The only meditation they refuse to do is the meditation that Jesus taught of in the parable of the sower and the seed. In that parable He warns that our life will not change beyond the degree of thought, study and meditation we give to what we hear![3]

Everyone meditates!

The heart is designed to protect you from outside influences. No one can change your heart but you. Neither positive thinking, nor affirmations, nor confessions will change your life unless your heart is involved. In fact, some studies indicate that positive thinking, affirmations and confessions actually create more stress, which would mean there is less likelihood of being able to influence you heart in a positive manner!

Your heart will resist all your efforts to change your sense of self apart from functioning the way you are wired to function…following the rules for transformation. It is no different than a computer system. You can have all the right components—the motherboard, the processors, the screen, the keyboard and everything else—but unless you follow the way they are designed to operate you will get nothing.

There are incredible books that give you tools and resources for success. But the missing component in every success book I have ever read is the heart. You can turn every book you've ever read from being a frustration to a gold mine when your heart has been established in success.

How does that happen? It happens by seeing, believing and experiencing yourself as a success.

Heart Physics® does not ask you to throw away everything you've learned, and it certainly doesn't imply that others are wrong. Heart Physics® supplies the missing component for every dimension of life, love, happiness, health and success. Heart Physics® takes what you have been doing your entire life for self-destruction and shows you how to use it to map out the future of your dreams!

People who use Heart Physics® find that it enhances and makes workable everything they have ever learned about success. It provides the one missing component: the rules and tools for transformation.

CHAPTER 12

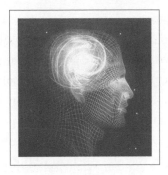

WHY I RESIST CHANGE

A moment of peace is more productive than a lifetime of worry.

CHANGE IS THE ONE constant in life, yet it is the one thing most resisted! Without continual change our life and mind begin to degenerate through stagnation. When we refuse to change in pace with a changing world, every day we become more out of touch with the world in which we live. We die to life, love and opportunity as it slowly slips through the rigid fingers of inflexibility! One of the prominent signs of death in any living organism is rigidity and inflexibility. That which becomes rigid is dying. That which is being infused with new life is always flexible.

The dynamic of change must be embraced for continual progress. Think of it like this. Every day the world around you changes. Your body is changing. Your family and its needs are changing. The marketplace is changing. Nothing is static. That which brought success yesterday was something that worked in a world that is now different. No matter how effective something was yesterday, the law of life demands that we change today or be left behind. No matter how similar today seems to yesterday, millions of variables have changed!

Change should and could be one of the great life adventures. The opportunity for personal growth presents a world of new opportunity, excitement and wonder. Maybe this is one of the many things to which Jesus was referring when He told us to remain as children! Every year in school we had to adapt, and as children we were willing. Every grade advancement demanded that we develop new skills, meet new people and venture into the unknown. When we get married we begin what should be one of the greatest adventures of change: two people adjusting enough to grow together as one. Likewise, business should be a world that compels us to embrace change! Success in any arena of life insists that we be like children, always flowing with the change. We must keep our hearts pliable with positive expectation, wonder and excitement!

The demand for change will be viewed as danger or opportunity, as threat or challenge, as adventure or risk! Upon close examination we see that the areas that present the greatest demand for growth and change are the areas that offer the greatest possibility of pleasure and reward. Those who focus on the reward find themselves continually motivated to grow, change and thrive! Sadly, some studies indicate that the two places people are most resistant to change are in personal relationships and finances, the two areas with the greatest potential for happiness and the greatest demand for change!

As we will discover, the ability to face personal change comfortably is based on our self-worth. Self-worth is one of the deepest mental/emotional filters through which we process and interpret everything in the outside world. Everything we view is seen through our personal perspective; our personal perspective is an extension of how we see ourselves. How we see anything is never exactly how it is; it is simply how we see it. When the view of ourselves changes, our view of the situation changes!

Change should and could be one of the great life adventures.

HEART VS. HEAD

Many powerful factors come into play when one is faced with change. The heart is designed to protect us from unwanted change. Unless a person used the "hard-wired" process for heart transformation, change will be impossible. God created (hard-wired) us to make our own choices and to bring about only the heart changes that we desire. The heart is the absolute root of our self-perception. What we believe about ourselves can be changed only by our own choices, following some fairly predictable guidelines. Sadly, people follow these guidelines by default to bring about negative change. Few people ever master them for positive change.

One of the most pronounced internal struggles when facing change of any kind is the struggle between the heart and the mind. The Bible is very clear about this struggle and poignantly points out the devastation of the carnal mind. The carnal mind is a mind that has been programmed by culture, religion and other environmental influences that resist the quality of life offered by God!

God leads from the heart, not the mind. True creativity, inspiration and even wisdom come from the heart, not the mind! The mind is all about what has been intellectually learned. The mind, which expresses itself through the brain, is great at gathering and observing the details. But our tendency to want to live out of our mind limits our capacity for success to our intellectual boundaries. In fact, the mind resists following the heart into the unknown realms of true creativity and inspiration. The unknown doesn't feel safe to the mind. Among other things it represents a loss of control. The mind needs for everything to be controlled within the bounds of previous experiences and intellectual judgments to maintain a false sense of security.

> *True creativity, inspiration and even wisdom come from the heart, not the mind!*

When a person is relaxed and at peace he or she has access to the heart, which has access to all the wisdom of God! When people are relaxed and peaceful creativity flows effortlessly. Complex problems that could not be solved intellectually become simple. Without training and experience few people ever develop the ability to stay at peace for very long. Sometimes our creative flood is reduced to a trickle when the conscious mind jumps into action and seeks to take control of the few precious drops of creativity that leaked past the confines of the mind.

The HeartMath Institute has done remarkable studies about the mind and the heart. Through their research they have reached the conclusion that every heartbeat is more than a mere wave. Within that wave is encoded information. It is believed that every time the heart beats it sends a wave of encoded information to the brain, to all the cells of the body and for an undefined distance around the body. Studies have been done to support these theories.[1]

There is some link between the physical heart and the spiritual heart. No one can define the boundaries or overlaps. But cutting-edge science is discovering that what the Bible had said about the heart for thousands of years is not just metaphoric; it is factual and scientific. Just as the Bible teaches we think with our heart and we think with our mind. The thoughts of the heart emerge effortlessly when we are at peace. The thoughts of the mind run almost non-stoppable, and the more troubled we become the more the mind runs it endless barrage of thoughts!

PRACTICE PEACE

Many different studies have identified the changes in the mind and body under stress. We know that when threatened the sympathetic nervous system takes over to put us in the fight or flight mode. In this mode, the blood stops nurturing the organs and is moved out to the limbs to make us ready for fight or flight. In this stressed state our organs are no longer being nurtured; our body has shifted into survival mode. We know that the habitual state of stress is the cause of nearly all disease. In the absence of stress the body is fully capable of healing itself and maintaining abundant health. However, under stress we destroy our bodies to ward off the threat, whether real or imagined.

What happens in the body is very similar to what happens in the heart and mind. Under stress the blood moves to a different part of the brain. The part of the brain that is activated is not connected to our sense of self. It doesn't really think about consequences. It has one mission: survival! Just as the body stops being nurtured under stress, the mind no longer receives the nurturing messages from the heart that carry the wisdom of God. It is even possible that the brain blocks the heart's signal. In this state we can destroy all that we value; self-existence overrides character, ethics and wisdom.

Most of the threats that put us in the fight or flight mode are more imagined than real. They are interpreted as threats by the mind, which always longs to be in control, always needs to know all the answers and desperately needs to stay within the bounds of the "known." Since success is always a venture into the unknown,

In the absence of stress the body is fully capable of healing itself and maintaining abundant health.

there is always going to be a degree of stress. Every individual will, from his or her sense of self, judge the stress as a threat of danger or the challenge of a new opportunity.

Once the mind has isolated us from the peaceful wisdom of the heart, the list of deceitful tactics that it employs are almost endless. The quests for more answers seems plausible until we realize that it is really a form of intellectual paralysis that does nothing more than justify inaction. The need to control the process feels safe until it sabotages all possibilities of success. The feelings of insecurity are misunderstood as warnings from the heart. But none of these will bring the success that comes from hearing the wisdom of God that comes from the heart.

Practice living in peace. Living in peace is more than removing chaos, although that's not a bad start. Peace is something that comes from the heart. Take time to relax every day. The reason for a Sabbath day was more for this aspect of man than all the religious activities that have been built around it. Taking regular time off will facilitate more creativity and result in more success than being a workaholic. Man was wired to live at rest—that is, peace! A major aspect of peace is relaxation. In fact, you will not enter into emotional peace if you are holding physical stress in your body. That's why learning to live in peace, which is an inner activity, starts with relaxation, which is an external activity.

You will not enter into emotional peace if you are holding physical stress in your body.

Make it a point to take "peace breaks" throughout the day. They don't have to be long; just a few minutes to become calm and relaxed. But even more importantly, when you feel yourself starting to become stressed, stop immediately and return to peace.

If you are in a place where you can do so, sit with your feet on the floor, legs uncrossed. With your head faced forward, roll your eyes upward and look at a spot high on the ceiling or the wall for a few seconds. This actually affects your brain waves. Then, when you are ready, close your eyes. Simply closing your eyes also slows your brain waves. Then breathe deeply and slowly in through your nose. Feel the breath go deep into your belly somewhere behind or slightly below the belly button, in the center of the body. Exhale slowly and evenly through slightly parted lips. This type of breathing affects the nervous system, causing a shift to the parasympathetic functions of nurturing. Abide in that place for a few moments, then acknowledge, "I am feeling stressed, but I don't want to. I now release all stress and tension and allow myself to be filled with the peace of God!" Think of anything positive, happy or enjoyable until you create some positive emotions. You'll be amazed how quickly you can change you physiological state and return to the place of peace. If you are in a meeting and are unable to do all the above, simply change your breathing. You can do it very subtly so no one will even notice.

When you have reached the place of peace, acknowledge that God gives you wisdom. Acknowledge that you are open and ready for a solution to the problem you face. The solution may come immediately or it may come at another time when you are relaxed, but be assured it will come.

As you view the stressful situation that has caused you to feel danger and to shift into fight or flight mode, your perspective will change. What looked like danger will now look like opportunity!

CHAPTER 13

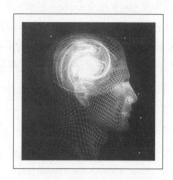

EXPANDING YOUR FINANCIAL BOUNDARIES

When your success exceeds your sense of self stress is inevitable!

N O MATTER HOW MUCH money a person is able to make, every individual has personal financial boundaries. It is the glass ceiling, the invisible wall that stops us just short of our goals. When hitting the ceiling some of us try to learn more information while others give up until they can find some means of temporary motivation. Some blame outside sources. Regardless of our reaction, the boundary will remain firmly in place until we deal with the real issue…our heart.

The Book of Proverbs tells us that the heart is the source of all boundaries.[1] People, circumstances and to a great degree even the economy are just places for us to focus blame. But as we all know, finding something to blame has never solved any of our problems. Excuses are the anchors that keep our vessels from sailing seamlessly through the waters of life! To move the boundaries we must address the beliefs of our heart.

WANT SUCCESS? CHANGE YOUR HEART

While I am a firm believer in motivation, most motivation doesn't work. In fact, motivation can become a source of internal stress and disillusionment. To get someone excited without solving the problem is like giving a cancer patient a pain pill. The person may feel healed momentarily, but as soon as the medication wears off the person is faced with the same problem. However, internal motivation that comes from seeing ourselves and our future differently is powerful and long lasting!

A change of heart always produces a change in our sense of self!

Keep in mind that beliefs of the heart are always directly connected to our sense of self. No tip, technique or plan touches my heart until I see myself differently. I have to see me working the plan. I have to take ownership both intellectually and emotionally or it still will be something that only exists in my intellectual world. A change of heart always produces a change in our sense of self!

Every belief is filtered through how we see ourselves. Therefore, even though beliefs can cause limitations in our life, they also are protecting us. When we experience any level of success that exceeds our sense of self it causes stress. As I mentioned before, the Chinese character that most closely relates to stress has a compound meaning: opportunity and danger. Stress is when we are faced with situations that we will turn into success or trouble, all based on the beliefs of our heart.

There is no static definition of opportunity. That which threatens one man stimulates an entrepreneurial motivation in another. What looks like the end for one looks like the beginning for another. The heart, which at the core is our sense of self, determines if the stressor is an opportunity or a danger based on what we believe about ourselves.

After losing everything I had, I landed in Huntsville, Alabama, with little more than the clothes on my back, a couch to sleep on and a stereo. I had just had a number of surgeries and was out of work, with no vehicle, no job and no known opportunities. A close friend who needed a place to live came along with me. I managed to borrow a few hundred dollars and a small truck to move my sparse possessions. We found an apartment with just enough money to pay the first month's rent and turn on the utilities.

As we stood in front of the rental office trying to make the final decision, my friend said, "We'll never make it! How will we make money? What happens if we can't come up with next month's rent?" I pulled out my calculator and added up the total number of hours we could work in a month and divided that by what it would cost to pay the rent utilities, groceries and a few necessities. It came to about 80 cents an hour. I turned to him and asked, "Can you make forty cents an hour?" He fired back, "Of course I can!" "Well, good, because that will cover your half of the expenses."

We rented the apartment and through a series of situations we started a small business. We started out renting a van. In a few weeks we made enough money to buy our own. We purchased new tools every time we got a new job and in less than three months we had a successful business providing us with a good living.

In about six months I moved on to another business. While this business was providing very well for us, it was not large enough to satisfy my sense of self. I knew this was just a bridge to get my feet on the ground and move forward. So I gave my share of the business to my friend and moved on. At that time the business, the van and all the tools were paid for and we had more work than we could do. But remember this is the person who was stretched to believe we could come up with rent and utilities.

Over the next few months I received repeated calls from the contractors who sub-contracted work to us. They all wanted me to come back into the business. You see, this level of success exceeded my friend's sense of self. It was just a matter of time until he had lost all of our contracts, sold the tools and the van, and was back where he started, with no place to live. He was a good man and a good worker. He was actually better at the craft than I, but the difference was how we saw ourselves.

IT'S ALL ABOUT THE BOUNDARIES

When faced with stress created by exceeding our sense of self, we tend to get into the survival mode, which means our decisions often lack ethics and values. Survival is not about ethics; it is about surviving. Anything can be justified when the feeling of survival guides our choices. The result of making compromising decisions always results in more conflict, guilt and yes…more stress! Ultimately, the survival decisions become part of the self-sabotage that brings our lives back into the boundaries that we can comfortably accept.

It would be like a man who marries a woman whom he believes is way out of his league. Because this is beyond his sense of self he could become jealous, controlling, possessive or even abusive. His discomfort (stress) drives him to make decisions that push his dream girl away from him. He tries to force the relationship; after all, it doesn't feel natural for him to have such a "catch." When he loses his dream girl, he creates some distorted logic about beautiful women and sets out to find a "plain Jane" who doesn't exceed his comfort zone!

We are wired to continually advance; however, we are programmed to establish boundaries that make us feel safe.

Whether we realize it or not, all forward advancement causes us to continually encounter the boundaries of our sense of self. We are wired to continually advance; however, we are programmed to establish boundaries that make us feel safe. When that uneasy feeling of surpassing our boundaries is realized we find some way to put on the brakes. We must, however, realize that seldom, if ever, do we have a conscious thought that says, "I've crossed my boundaries." Generally we just feel stressed. That stress will be interpreted as danger or opportunity.

I once had a friend approach me about his invisible ceiling. Every time his business reached a certain point, it would blow up. Things would go wrong, and he would find his business dwindling back down to the level that he had come to accept as his normal. Then he got a great opportunity for advancement. He saw the potential for both danger and opportunity.

He had heard me talk about the heart and the power of our beliefs and boundaries. He realized that unless he changed his heart, he would turn this great opportunity into massive disaster that eventually would land him back at his "normal success." We spent an afternoon discussing the power of heart beliefs and he spent a few hours using a couple of Heart Physics® tools. In just one afternoon he moved his boundaries. He has ultimately surpassed any level of success he had ever imagined. Those who have a heart for it, grow with the opportunities. Those who do not grow subconsciously sabotage their success so they can remain within the bounds of their current comfort zone—that is, how they see themselves!

A stuck state is nothing more than a boundary of the heart.

Regardless of how well-adjusted we are or how entrepreneurial we think, we all will, at one time or another, hit a "stuck state." A stuck state is that place where we just cannot move forward no matter how hard we try. When we hit our boundaries problems will come from anywhere and everywhere. We can get sick, have an accident, lose our best employees or have an overthrow by a partner or employee. It all seems inexplicable, but it is just the workings of the heart. When we consider the source of the obstacles we create a logic that makes us feel comfortable with our limitations, but it is just a stuck state. A stuck state is nothing more than a boundary of the heart.

Through the Heart Physics® we equip you with simple-to-use heart tools that make it possible for you to expand the boundaries of your heart. This is not a program to teach people how to make money; this is a program for people on every level of the financial scale who want to move past where they are. You may make a million dollars each year, but if you're stuck, you have to move the boundaries. You probably don't need to learn a new technique. Most people already know enough to succeed beyond their wildest dreams. Knowledge is not the problem. Beliefs are the problem.

Go to any bookstore and you will find hundreds of books on success. Some are considered Christian and some are considered secular. Some are nothing more than get-rich schemes, while some are filled with great advice. However, the frustration of a person who studies success is not in his or her inability to learn and even apply the information. The struggle is in the inability to move the boundaries so that a new level of success can be sustainable. Those who create sustaining wealth without stress are not the ones who become masters of finance; they are the ones who become masters of change.

CHAPTER 14

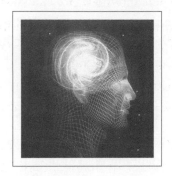

CREATING SUSTAINABLE SUCCESS

Making money is a skill, being successful is an identity.

THERE IS SUCCESS THAT comes as individual experiences, and then there is the person who is a success. The two may look much alike on the outside. And for all practical purposes they both temporarily share the same benefits. But one is an achievement while the other is a state of being. Where the two begin to look very different is when one seeks to sustain success or duplicate his or her success in a new endeavor!

A person can have an individual success without ever becoming a truly successful person. Such a person can have a job where he or she earns a good salary. He may inherit a business. Or, she may have struck on an idea that was needed in the marketplace. Any of these would be acceptable and at least two of the three would be admirable. But these types of successes in no way ensure that the individual can duplicate his or her success in a new venture.

Real success is a state, not a goal. A goal is something you reach through work and effort. A state is an internal realm people enter based on the way they perceive themselves. The person who *is* a

> **Real success is a state, not a goal.**

99

success, internally, will have many shared characteristics with others who are truly successful. The person who has *had* a success may discover his or her inability to duplicate that success in another market. It's like the one-hit wonders from the 1960s who had one great hit song and were never again able to put a song on the charts!

TWO CORE BELIEFS

Someone has said that the common denominator among successful people is flexibility and adaptability! While I have observed and reached the same conclusion, I also have seen that flexibility and adaptability are facilitated by deeper personal traits. To be flexible and adaptable one must be comfortable with change…change in procedures, change in techniques, acquisition of new skills and quite often personal character growth. These capabilities are facilitated by two even deeper core beliefs: self-worth and self-confidence! Self-worth says, "I am worthy of success." Self-confidence says, "I know I can achieve success!" (Obviously self-worth and self-confidence involve much more than this, but in seeking to apply these characteristics to success I have limited the scope of the definition here.)

Self-worth is the product of how I feel about me as a person. Self-confidence, however, comes from my track record. Self-confidence answers these questions: Do I finish what I start? Have I earned success in the past? And do I trust my skills and my ability to learn new skills? These two characteristics provide a foundation for sustainable and replicable success!

So often the people who have had only one success do not possess these traits. They are dismayed and perplexed when they are unable to sustain their success or duplicate it in other markets. Sadly, the route taken by those looking to expand their sustainable success does not include exercises of the heart. Too often a motivational seminar and excitability are taken as the indicator that they are ready for a new venture. But they find themselves hitting the glass ceiling again and again.

All sustainable success requires change at some level. To succeed at that which I have never done I must think and believe differently and acquire new skills. To continue with the same beliefs and skills will keep me

All sustainable success requires change at some level.

at my current levels of success. What's worse, if the demands of my job or business change, staying at the same skill and belief level may be the cause of failure in my present endeavor. Adaptability isn't just a prerequisite for a new endeavor; it is essential for maintaining success in a changing market.

Dr. Stephen Covey wrote the massively successful bestseller, *The 7 Habits of Highly Effective People*. In the first chapter he talks about his research into success material that has been written over the past 200 years. For the first 150 years success books emphasized the need to develop character, ethics and other personal traits. But over the past 50 years, according to his research, the majority of books about success have emphasized quick fixes, formulas and gimmicks.[1] There has been the delusion that true success could be achieved and sustained independent of personal growth. The result is evident in our current economy and the corruption that took us down this path.

Today motivational seminars abound. Every year millions of dollars are spent on motivational seminars and books. While I am a proponent of such material, I also realize that those who develop their mind but do not develop their heart will have little more than massive frustration to show for all their effort. When our success exceeds our character our success becomes our destruction!

According to Dr. George Kappas, positive thinking only works for about 15 percent of the population.[2] According to some studies, positive affirmation actually causes more stress.[3] Why would positive, healthy, needful input have a negative effect? Simple! If you don't really believe in your heart what you are saying, your mind perceives it to be a lie, not an affirmation!

WHAT LIMITS SUCCESS?

One of the greatest limitations to our success is the fact that we study and become comfortable with the ideas of success, but are completely uncomfortable with the proposition of personal change. Our self-worth perceives the need to change as a form of rejection or self-criticism. Studying success techniques without the willingness to make the needed personal changes is like finding a city filled with treasure but having no bridge to get there. Personal transformation is the bridge that takes us to the next level of success. All sustainable success beyond our current boundaries requires personal development—that is, change! Change happens when people feel safe and non-threatened! This only occurs in a heart established in healthy self-worth.

Personal transformation is the bridge that takes us to the next level of success.

People who study success often become frustrated at their inability to get what they learn to work. Too often we search for a change in skills without a change in thoughts and beliefs. Although skills can certainly make us move a little further down the line, without self-worth we will still hit the invisible barrier. Those who become comfortable with personal change and master the art of transformation easily make what they learn to work! They understand that enduring financial success is the result of personal growth.

The weaknesses that work against us to make change difficult are the same strengths that work for us when our heart beliefs are healthy and positive. Our heart resists change that is not approached though certain clearly defined processes. Any time we entertain the possibility of change, powerful protective forces come into play. The same forces that help us hold to our healthy beliefs help us hold to our destructive beliefs.

Our heart is designed so that we can be influenced only by ourselves. No outside source, neither God nor man, can influence our heart without our cooperation. This protective capacity is designed to make it impossible for our beliefs to be changed without our cooperation. It is this very capability of the heart that protects the truth we believe. However, it is this same protective capacity that keeps us bound to that which is not true! The limiting beliefs about our success are guarded by the workings of our heart unless we use the tools God gave us to bring about heart change!

So the problem is clear. When I have destructive beliefs it is very difficult for me to get the help I need. My heart is designed to hold the beliefs it currently has regardless of how damaging they are. It relentlessly resists new beliefs regardless of how promising they are. The way I'm wired causes me to desire progress but my life programming causes me to resist change! By understanding the process of transformation, coupled with the effective heart tools, thousands of people have used Heart Physics® to easily and comfortably bring about the desired changes.

Don't misunderstand; I am not telling you that change should be hard or impossible. No! Just the opposite! Change is actually quite easy when we use the proper tools. Resistance to change should not lead us to believe it is hard; it simply should be seen as an indicator that we

Change is actually quite easy when we use the proper tools.

have not followed the rules for transformation. When we follow the rules of transformation change can be easy and enjoyable.

Self-worth is the key factor in whether change is perceived as a danger or an opportunity. As discussed previously, change causes stress and stress is perceived as either danger or opportunity. In a meeting with a dear friend, who had been locked into years of destructive behavior, I was delighted to hear her share her new life views.

During the previous year we had worked together to help her cross her incredible, seemingly immovable life boundaries. As a result of personal heart work, she looked at this boundary that previously had been seen as a great danger and now saw it as the greatest opportunity for growth. In the same way, by applying the proper tools, the boundary that had previously rendered us paralyzed and frightened can now be approached with limitless hope and unreasonable joy.

PERSONAL DEVELOPMENT IS KEY

As previously mentioned, there is success that occasionally occurs that exceeds our sense of self. Success that exceeds our sense of self creates stress, tension, fear, worry and a host of other destructive emotions. Thus the wisdom of God's Word: *"The prosperity of fools shall destroy them."*[4] I often meet people who succeed at something. Maybe they started a business that makes it, or they have a good paying job. They may have been at the right place at the right time, or they may just be hard workers. This in no means takes away from their legitimate success. But these can be the types of successes that come because of one particular skill or unique opportunity.

To have the types of success that do not require personal development can be seductive. It often can make you feel that you know more than you really know! For example, I recall working with a man who had built a very successful service-oriented business. He was no doubt a hard worker. He wanted to relocate and start another business. Sadly, he thought because he had one success that he was an entrepreneur. After attempting several failed businesses and some bad investments he discovered that he did not have the skills or the self-worth to venture into these untested waters.

Sadly he was surrounded by people who could have helped him to become a monumental success, but the proof of his self-worth was exposed by his refusal to objectively consider advice from qualified people. His lack of self-confidence was revealed in two areas: how fast he gave up and his intimidation of learning new skills.

As much as I hate to compare people who have succeeded at anything to those who win the lottery, there are often some uncanny similarities. They both discover that having money without personal development creates unsustainable wealth! The single skill that brought them their current level of success was not enough to take them out into new arenas. However, those who develop themselves in the process of their current successes are always poised to step out into the next venture that takes them to the next level.

We can create a degree of financial security by having a good paying job. Or, we can have a degree of success by meeting a need in the marketplace. As far as that goes we can get an inheritance and be made instantly wealthy. But the ability to

The ability to sustain financial success apart from personal development is rare.

sustain financial success apart from personal development is rare. Sustainable success is nearly always the result of a combination of character and skills development, which is an expression of flexibility and adaptability, which are the fruit of self-worth and self-confidence.

Self-worth comes from feeling loved. The biblical definition of love is value. Although people can contribute to our self-worth, nothing other than knowing and feeling the incredible love—the value that God has for us—can give us an unchanging sense of self. Heart Physics® Essentials is designed to meet this, the greatest need of mankind. In 30 days of Heart Physics® Essentials people experience an entirely new sense of self.

Make loving God and loving people a new priority. Learning to give and receive love with both people and God is the road to self-worth. This is the core of all healthy life emotions. The person who can give and receive love has found the endless fountain of self-worth!

Self-confidence is the product of one's track record. If you don't have a good track record, start building one. Keep your commitments. Let your word mean something. Show up on time for appointments. Before you agree to do anything think it through to make sure you have counted the cost. Then follow it through to the end of your responsibilities. Give up all justifications and blame-shifting for past failures.

Pursue character development. Write a couple of pages describing yourself with the type of character you really want to have. Review it and commit yourself to the pursuit of those traits every day. Be the person you want to be.

CHAPTER 15

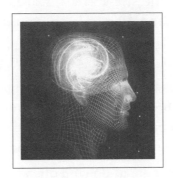

CONTROLLING THE PROCESS

Success always takes us down a path we have never walked.

THE CAUSES OF FAILING are abundant; the cures are pretty simple: Develop the skills, live in peace, listen to your heart! The problem with many of the failure factors is the deceptive comfort and false peace they bring. The absence of stress does not equate the presence of peace.

There are two types of motivation. Our life programming has made us more susceptible to one or the other. The ideal is a healthy combination of both. One type is "away from motivation," which is driven primarily by the fear of pain. "Away from motivation" means the main driving force in our life is the attempt to avoid pain. The second type is "toward motivation." "Toward motivation" is when we are compelled to move in a direction because we are trying to move toward pleasure.

When peace is not one's habitual state then "away from motivation," the attempt to avoid pain, can become the dominant motivation. When the closest thing we know to peace is the absence of conflict we will more readily withdraw from stressful situations. But remember, every opportunity has a degree of stress. "Away from motivation" can set off a cascade of

Every opportunity has a degree of stress.

subconscious motivational factors that interpret the stress as a threat instead of an opportunity and drive us in the opposite direction.

We must remember that every "unknown" is considered a threat. A threat produces fear. Fear creates stress. Stress puts us into fight or flight. Fight or flight makes it virtually impossible to hear the intuitive, creative voice of the heart. Fight or flight sets off a barrage of physiological and emotional responses that are never conducive to thriving, just surviving!

Success will always take us down paths we have never been, accomplishing a new goal or living a bigger dream. The desire to grow and expand—that is, to succeed—is inherent in humankind. We were wired for success. From the first man until now there has been an inner compelling to exercise dominion over planet Earth, to subdue and succeed! Man as he was originally designed (wired) is an inherent dreamer. We imagine a better life. Einstein said, "Imagination is more important than knowledge. Knowledge is limited." There is no limitation to the imagination. That imagination is the seed from which all new success grows. But, since it is imagined, that means it may not yet be real to us. A new venture may have many similarities to past successes but there are always unknowns.

FAILURE FACTORS

There are two types of failure. There are people who play it safe. They never venture out or run the risk. These people have been programmed to avoid pain and disappointment by simply not trying! They are dominated by "away from motivation." Then there are those who launch out but experience the painful disappointment of not reaching their goal. These are usually people dominated by "toward motivation." These people are probably not developing the needed skills or the essential self-worth to grow beyond their current boundaries.

Too often we analyze our failures from our despair and reach completely inaccurate conclusions. An inaccurate conclusion is like a wrong diagnosis from a doctor. We may proceed with all manner of quality treatments, but they are the wrong treatments for our sickness, which in turn pave the way for future challenges. Sometimes failure factors are obvious, easily identifiable external factors like not having enough capital, needing employees with a different skills set or marketing failures.

Some of the failure factors can, however, be quite subtle because they have more to do with internal factors than external ones. Sometimes the thing we did that produced failure was the sabotage of succeeding beyond our sense of self. It is hard to identify internal beliefs as the cause for failure just by using mere intellectual observation. Intellectual observation is usually a self-judgment imposed by the mind's need for control. Regardless of the internal source, conscious evaluation will never bring us to the true conclusion. Only heart tools like those in Heart Physics® can help us understand the workings of the heart. Heart tools take us past the control of the mind and to the core beliefs that subconsciously run our lives.

Conscious evaluation will never bring us to the true conclusion. Only heart tools can help us understand the workings of the heart.

One of the most common failure factors that thwart change is our attempt to control the process! All too often we experience real inspiration and see a clear goal and then fall into this most deceptive ploy. In order to avoid the "unknowns" presented by a new success venture, we seek to create some sense of security. In our need to feel comfortable we attempt to find a new destination while following an old map! We pretend to strive for the goal but actually put the priority of comfort ahead of the outcome. In other words, we take control of the process! We make it look like something we've done before, something that makes us feel safe.

Keep in mind, any new success requires a new path. After all, if we knew how to have the level of success we desired, we would already have it. If we knew the way, we would have already made the journey. New success is always an adventure into the unknown. Granted, there are certain aspects of the journey that can be studied and planned, but there are countless aspects of the voyage that will be totally unknown until it is time to take the step.

Any new success requires a new path.

This may be the reason for the formula craze that has dominated both the business and the religious literature for the past 50 years. Formulas don't require us to listen to our heart. They require no thinking, no creativity and no unknowns! Formulas offer a static map to every new destination based on the similarities of the desired outcome. But, there isn't a one-size-fits-all formula for success.

Think of the people who come out of a bad relationship. They meet a new person and without giving it a thought they follow the same path in this relationship that they did in the one that failed. They know they want love; they know they want happiness. In fact, because of past hurts, they want it more than ever. But they never consider that the way they approached the previous relationship may be why it failed. Or, they never consider that this person may be totally different from the previous person. They are pursuing a new love following the same process.

The same thing happens in parenting. We look back at all the things our parents did to us. We sometimes spend years going through therapy trying to overcome our dysfunction. Then when we have children we follow the same path our parents followed. Why? Do we think it will work? No! We follow it because it is "known"!

In the same way in our path to success we destroy new inspiration by following the only path that is familiar to us. We choose the known by default. We don't question or think about it. We follow the known because it is safe. We follow the known to keep from feeling threatened, but mostly we follow the known because we don't think and consider. We don't listen to the voice of our heart. In fact, we often resist the voice of our heart, especially if we are desperate. Desperation puts us in one of those modes where our mind takes over and seeks to silence the wisdom of the heart. Its ultimate goal is not to find a new success but to keep us on a familiar path.

Because of the heart's role in all of life's major issues, there can be no cookie cutter approach. No one has the same background. Each of us struggle with our own confidence and self-worth issues. Although we all may use the same tools to deal with our heart, at the end of the process we will have to walk the path that best facilitates our heart's capacity for success. There will be similar steps, but how and when to take them is completely individualized by the multitude of factors from our own past as well as the present core beliefs that shape our faith.

FOLLOW THE PATH OF PEACE

If we stay at peace we can trust our own heart to lead us into the path we can follow. If we trust God as our Shepherd, then we will have Him as the one familiar constant that we know we can trust and, according to the Psalm 23:1, He will always lead us away from lack. *"The Lord is my shepherd; I shall not want* [lack].*"* People with their heart at peace allow the wisdom of God to emerge *as* they walk the path, not before they walk the path. I realize that we need to plan. There are some details we must have in advance. But the things we need in advance will unfold before us just as the things we need to find along the way will unfold. Life becomes a perfect blend of planning and spontaneity, knowing and not knowing, but feeling safe no matter where we are in the journey.

Asking for wisdom before starting a new journey is much safer than insisting that we know. Few things blind us to reality more than insisting we see! When our cup is full it cannot receive anything other than what it presently holds. But an empty cup is ready to receive the fresh nectar of life. When we think we know is when we cannot see past our current

Wise people know what they know, but keep their heart open to discover what they do not know.

level of knowledge. It's all right to know that we know some things; however, wise people know what they know, but maybe as important, they keep their heart open to discover what they do not know.

When seeking a new success, have times of peaceful planning. Peaceful planning is not where you are in a room full of people brainstorming, which I think can and should be done. Peaceful planning is where you take all the information from planning and brainstorming and you hit the pause button. In other words, you do something very relaxing. Gather all the facts, then ask for wisdom! Rather than sitting and waiting for wisdom to immediately come, find something really enjoyable or relaxing to do that has nothing to do with the decision you need to make. When you are ready, sit silently, relaxing, breathing deeply. Enter your Heart Zone and allow wisdom to emerge. Proceed with what you know and trust the rest will follow. But above all stay in peace. When you don't know what to do resist the temptation to default to what is familiar. If you do find yourself moving to what is familiar, do a quick relaxation exercise and notice how you feel in your heart about that move. Let peace be the referee that gives you the red or green light. Until you find peace, don't proceed!

CHAPTER 16

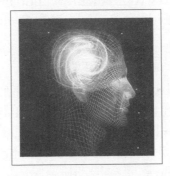

FAILURE FEELINGS

Feelings may have little to do with the reality that exists, but
everything to do with the reality you create!

EVERYONE WANTS TO IMPROVE the quality of his or her life. Just ask anyone! Millions of dollars are spent every year on success, self-help and self-development material. People read self-help books, attend seminars and apply principles of positive thinking. But in the end all the effort seems to produce only limited temporary results.

Today the most common ads you'll receive that promise to teach you the latest self-help or personal development insights will include a very persuasive reference to the fact that you've tried things that just don't work. The unspoken common knowledge of the entire self-help industry is, "This isn't working like we thought it would." Developers are racing to find the missing ingredient in personal growth because, in theory, what is being taught should work!

The confusion is often created by the fact that a particular program will work for some but be totally ineffective in others. Because it works for one, the natural assumption is that it should work for all. This very mind-set feeds into the precise reason it doesn't work for some: self-worth! The moment I declare, "This works for everyone," my message defaults to, "If it doesn't work for you, it's your fault!" So another weight is added to the already overpowering negative emotions that limit your success.

IT TAKES TWO

Behavior alone is never the key to abiding success.

One of the greatest early studies in success was based on an idea like this one: "If we find someone who made a million dollars and do what he did, we too would make a million dollars." Although I read those books and encourage others to do so, I realize there are deeper internal issues that must be duplicated along with the external efforts. Behavior alone is never the key to abiding success. It is not simply what people did that made them successful; it is *how* and *why* they did it. All of the external actions were supported by a set of internal beliefs.

Although there are many common denominators in any success that can be easily learned and duplicated, there are also millions of possible variables, many of which have to be in play for the external efforts to produce replicable results. Outward action must be supported by internal beliefs, thoughts and feelings or the outcome will not be the same. Beliefs are the emotional fuel that gives life to our external actions.

The rule of macrocosm-microcosm helps bring us to clear understanding. Those who embrace a random theory of "creation" fail to understand the wisdom that has been prevalent in every ancient civilization. The Chinese, the Jews, Christians and many other ancient cultures believe in a creation that was brought into being and is held together by an intelligent logic. All things therefore follow the same logic. The accurate understanding of these life principles gives us truth that can be applied across the board in every arena of life!

In the world of physics we have spent hundreds of years having our interpretation of the physical world ruled by Newtonian physics. Then we had a secondary wisdom enter the scientific world: quantum physics.

114

Based on who you listen to, either side could sound right. But as in most pursuits of knowledge, the answer was not found in one extreme. The answer to physics is revealed when there is a combination of both sciences. Newtonian physics applies in the world of matter and large objects, but quantum physics applies in the subatomic, unseen world.

The same principles apply in the world of success and self-development. To simply duplicate actions would bring a limited degree of the desired results. It would be like applying Newtonian physics with total disregard for the quantum realities. To simply apply the internal workings would likewise produce certain desired outcomes. But those outcomes would be limited because of the application of only quantum physics. Just as the Bible talks about faith and works being able to produce predictable results, so too with physics, success and all that applies to life there must be a combination of the internal and the external. One of the key scriptures that help us understand this principle is, *"Faith without works is dead."*[1] The application of internal or external truth to the exclusion of the other will never produce the desired results.

THE KEY ISSUE: SELF-WORTH

At the core of our internal beliefs is the issue of self-worth. Self-worth manifests in every dimension of life. Every decision, every thought and every aspiration is subtly guided by our sense of self-worth. Every decision we make is done in a way that keeps us within the bounds of our current sense of self. Any decision that falls short of or exceeds our sense of self creates stress. We respond to stress with thrive or survive. In other words, we turn it into an opportunity and take the steps to develop our sense of self, or we see it as a danger and withdraw to stay within the boundaries of our limiting sense of self.

The invisible boundaries of my success are directly related to my self-worth. Ironically, there are those who seek success to prove their self-worth. These people are the ones who acquire, grow and outwardly appear to be a true success, only to experience humiliation, failure or loss as a result of their expansion. Remember, "success" that is not holistic will always cost you more than you can pay in the areas of health, relationships, spirituality and happiness.

Among the many subtle nuances of self-worth is the issue of worthiness. Worthiness manifests in many different failure feelings. Regardless of the individual feeling, the question always gets down to one issue: "Do I deserve success?" These are the four top failure feelings I encounter when working with those seeking to move their financial boundaries. "I am uncomfortable charging a fair price. I am not comfortable asking for a commitment. I fail to follow healthy business protocol. Why do I always trust the wrong people?"

The question always gets down to one issue: "Do I deserve success?"

Those whose self-worth issues flood over into the arena of worthiness are unconsciously and negatively driven by feeling they are unworthy of success. Therefore they are tremendously uncomfortable taking some of the steps that are very acceptable in any business dealings. This core feeling is made apparent when they have an inability to charge a fair price for their labors. This tendency is usually masked as generosity and is rewarded in our culture, but it is not rewarded in our income. When these people are self-employed, they seldom fail for a lack of work. Rather, they fail for a lack of resources. The inability to charge a fair price is a direct reflection of a lack of value for themselves!

Another place where unworthiness expresses itself is in the inability to ask people to make the needed commitments. I have seen many a young salesperson do an impeccable presentation but when it came time to close the deal they just could not ask for the commitment. Besides closing the deal, this difficulty also hinders the ability to require good business commitments along the process. Assumptions are made about the other person's intentions or loyalties. The person who does not feel worthy is too uncomfortable to ask for and then enforce commitments. This issue then bleeds over into the unwillingness to follow healthy business protocol like putting agreements in writing and the use of contracts.

The failure in these areas all too often results in trusting the wrong people. Trusting the wrong people is both a symptom and a cause. If I followed healthy business protocol, I would eliminate those who have less than admirable motives. But as a cause, it is highly possible that I am always attracted to the wrong people. Whether a symptom or a cause, by overcoming the first three of the failure feelings, this fourth problem is resolved. Feelings of unworthiness may be the primary reason smart, capable people either fail to accomplish their goals or seem to be taken advantage of so often. Implementation of these failure feelings are the subconscious raising of the boundaries that prevent us from succeeding beyond our sense of self. Whether we are contending with these feelings or seeing ourselves taking the destructive actions, we should take it as a red flag that we are venturing beyond our success boundaries. Before moving forward we should do the needed heart work to facilitate greater success.

SPIRITUALITY CANNOT BE IGNORED

It seems that many of the true innovators of self-help have come to recognize worthiness as a core internal condition for holistic success. There are all manner of programs to help people come to a sense of worthiness. However, to remove worthiness from self-worth is like pulling the teeth from a lion. He has a big roar, but in the end he is very limited! The problem with addressing the worthiness issue on a grander scale is that it forces us to deal with spiritual issues that are often not copacetic in the business world. This may explain why the past 50 years of success writing has been primarily gimmicks and formulas. When we remove spirituality and values there's nothing left but shortcuts.

Our spirituality—our conscious connection to God—is the core factor in self-worth and worthiness.

Despite the call for political correctness, our spirituality—our conscious connection to God—is the core factor in self-worth and worthiness. All thoughts, feelings and emotions stem from one of two roots: fear or love. Love, more than anything else, says, "I am valuable." Fear says, "I expect things to go wrong." It is a general sense of dread. That dread emerges from a negative sense of self.

The word *fear* used in the Scriptures to juxtapose against love comes from the root word *phobia*. Phobia is different from fear. Fear is the apprehension or dread that one feels based on fact. If you were bitten by a dog as a child, when you encounter a dog as an adult, you may have fear or apprehension. But this fear is based on fact. Phobia, however, is from an unknown, unexplainable source. It is a generalized dread that emerges from an unknown reason.

Feelings of unworthiness can stem from many sources. People who live in lack in their formative years often accept the feeling of lack as something that defines them as a person. If a person has unresolved ethical or moral failures, at a very deep level he or she can feel unworthy of future success. Sadly, many religious concepts incorporate ascetic philosophies that equate poverty with spirituality.

There may be nothing as powerful at creating core beliefs as those beliefs connected to our religious roots. Our puritanical cultural roots lend themselves to the idea that success should be difficult. Wealth is corruption. Success only belongs to those who have paid a great enough price. These ascetic-based philosophies will either keep us from success or keep us questioning ourselves every step of our journey toward our goals.

Do you find yourself struggling with these or other failure feelings? Are you constantly trying to overcome the sense of dread or expectation of failure? Is your background conducive to feelings of unworthiness? Do you have a hard time asking for commitments? Do you feel uncomfortable charging a fair price for your labors? Are you too intimidated to put agreements in writing? Do you come from a religious background than condemns wealth and success? Have you had a moral failure that still plagues you with guilt or shame? Do you repeatedly trust the wrong people? These are the warning signs!

If you answer yes to any of the above, you may have discovered the core obstacle to your success. Keep reading success books, keep attending seminars and developing your skills. But now you can take the quantum leap and deal with the root of your core issue. Resolve any of the issues you can on a conscious level, but determine what kind of heart work will bring the greatest change to your core beliefs and get started. You could be just days away from expanding your success boundaries!

One of the most powerful tools I have ever used to help people move past their limiting core beliefs is a Heart exercise called Limiting Beliefs. Limiting Beliefs is a short exercise that helps you identify the source of your limiting beliefs, remove them and install new productive beliefs in about 25 minutes. Go to www.Heartphysics.com to more information about this and other Heart Physics® tools.

CHAPTER 17

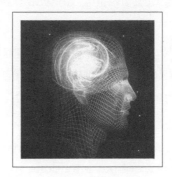

IDENTIFYING BOUNDARIES

Change your beliefs and your life will follow!

I T IS USUALLY QUITE easy to identify the place where our success "stalls." There may be an annual income that creates your financial ceiling. There may be a numeric growth indicator that you know will be your undoing. But as most of us can surely attest, identifying the location of the boundary and identifying the underlying beliefs that cause that boundary are worlds apart.

Most attempts to intellectually identify a heart boundary only result in a continuation of the problem. My intellectual attempt to identify my core problem is usually a self-judgment, which amounts to little more than a shot in the dark. If the problem could be identified intellectually, then it could be solved intellectually; therefore, I would have already solved it.

KNOW THE DIFFERENCE

Jesus gave us some incredible wisdom when He cautioned against attempting to pull up the tares from our field.[1] In this parable, an enemy sowed tares among the wheat. A tare was a plant that in its beginning stages looked just like wheat. Like all weeds, though, it leached the soil of nutrients and reduced the quality and quantity of the wheat crop. So, intellectually, the most practical thing to do would be to pull out everything we think to be a tare.

> *Regardless of the purity of our intentions, we really would not be able to tell the difference between the wheat and the tares.*

The problem with this logic is the self-destructive journey it would induce. Regardless of the purity of our intentions, we really would not be able to tell the difference between the wheat and the tares. Wheat and tares, like our limiting beliefs, cannot be intellectually differentiated. They look just alike until we see the fruit, or in other words, the consequences. Our inability to identify the difference would end in the destruction of the precious wheat. An intellectual evaluation of the faulty beliefs in our life causes us to follow the same self-destructive action Jesus warned against. Remember, until we become comfortable living from our heart we will always be more comfortable following the logic of the mind. By entering our Heart Zone we can identify limiting beliefs without the corruption and confusion of the intellectual mind.

Even if we "luck up" and identify our faulty core beliefs, they can never be changed while in an intellectual state of mind. Heart beliefs are corrected by accessing the realm of the heart. Some experts believe that in order to change a belief we have to enter the same state we were in when we accepted the belief. Although I'm sure that would be the easiest way, it is not the only way. I've spent years searching for and developing the powerful Heart Physics® tools. These Heart tools are those techniques that give us access to our heart. Some are very simple; some are very complex. Regardless, however, of the tool I use to bring about the change, it matters little if I haven't identified the belief I want to put off and chosen the belief I desire to put on in its place!

WATCH FOR SIGNS

The closest we can come to intellectually identifying our boundaries is by observing the things that occur repeatedly. Anything that occurs repeatedly without conscious effort is the result of a heart belief. In some way our sense of self is kept intact by the reoccurring failure. But that still does not tell us what we believe or where the belief came from.

A pastor who had all the needed skills to grow a successful church found himself repeatedly reaching a numeric plateau. His limitations really made no sense in light of his skills and his other life successes. Beliefs of the heart, however, are

> *Anything that occurs repeatedly without conscious effort is the result of a heart belief.*

never based on rational information. They are often an irrational combination of information and emotion. He would put forth effort, grow, hit the barrier, fall back, regroup, assert himself and soon find himself repeating the cycle. He had no problem recognizing his boundary. Likewise, he had no problem realizing it was a heart belief, but without identifying the actual limiting belief the solution would be very slow coming if not unattainable.

In just a few minutes of heart work aimed at identifying the beginning of this faulty belief, the source was found. The old belief was put off and a new belief was chosen and put on. In his case it had been the derogatory words of a grammar school principal that had been the seed that grew into a lifelong sense of self, creating an intellectually immovable boundary.

Many times we don't recognize a limiting belief until we launch out in a quest for new levels of success. I really believe this is the plight of many who utilize motivational programs without the assistance of the appropriate heart work. The motivation does its job—it moves them out of the place of comfort and inaction that has defined their current levels of success. As they move forward, though, the motivation is overcome by negative feelings and they become demotivated. The first signs of limiting beliefs usually appear in feelings of uneasiness, fear or inordinate discomfort.

SOME PRACTICAL TOOLS

One of our earliest Heart Physics® tools that I have used the most is a simple exercise called "Limiting Beliefs." It is designed to help us identify the limiting belief, uninstall the belief and install a new one. By identifying the actual belief, putting it off and replacing it with a new belief, the change is dramatic and almost instant. By following this with other tools that reinforce new thoughts and new behavior the new belief takes immediate shape.

Most of our core beliefs were established when we were children. That is the reason they are often so illogical. When we were children occurrences happened in our lives that produced strong emotion. We made a judgment as to why it was happening. As children we interpret the world around us as if all things are about us. The event creates the emotion, the judgment gives us the information and as children we add our irrational commentary.

Permanent change in any area is always one belief away!

By revisiting this event as an adult with new beliefs, new tools and new choices we are able to incorporate new responses to things that occurred in the past. In minutes we can open the prison door that has held us captive all our life. Permanent change in any area is always one belief away!

At the first symptom of a limiting belief we can take preemptive action. Don't wait until you face an actual failure. Don't create chaos that is too difficult to resolve. When the symptoms occur take action. Sometimes previewing can help us identify limiting beliefs. Through meditation we have the ability to experience an event before it actually happens. In our Heart Zone we allow ourselves to test the waters without really making the journey. As we have known for years, the mind cannot tell the difference between reality and a clearly imagined occurrence. As we imagine ourselves experiencing a goal we will identify the associated emotions.

Through the exercise of previewing we can walk through every aspect of a situation. By utilizing subtle heart tools we will feel safe and objective enough to recognize the feelings that emerge and very often the beliefs that are driving those feelings. We can then do the "Limiting Beliefs" exercise and put off the limiting belief and put on a new empowering belief.

One exercise that can be done right now before you venture out and even run the risk of encountering negative feelings or actual failure is a Personal Success Inventory. A Personal Success Inventory lists many of the most common limiting beliefs related to success. You can check yourself on each possible issue and immediately identify a variety of limiting beliefs. By the time you complete the list you will be able to add your own questions and expand this into others areas of life. (See Appendix A.)

Applied Kinesiology (AK) is a form of diagnosis using muscle testing as a primary feedback mechanism. AK works from the perspective that the body becomes strengthened when it is exposed to something that is good for it and becomes weakened when exposed to something that is bad for it. Likewise, it responds to that which is true or untrue for the individual being tested.

Applied Kinesiology is not an exact science. There is great debate about its accuracy. I have observed and used it for more than 20 years. I have seen chiropractors and other medical practitioners correctly identify and treat illnesses with incredible accuracy utilizing this internally wired tool. Likewise, I have seen people totally misuse and over-exaggerate its viability. The greatest temptation in AK is the tendency to attempt to control the outcome.

One of the common names for Applied Kinesiology is Muscle Testing. It works on a very simple manner. A person would read a statement as if it were true. Then a second person would test the strength of the first person's muscles to see if he had become weak or remained strong. The arm and/or the thumb and middle finger are the most common muscles I have seen used.

It starts by making sure you are hydrated. Remove metal jewelry and glasses. While standing with feet together, raise your dominant arm to shoulder height, parallel to the floor. The person testing you would stand directly in front of you. Using two fingers she would push down at the wrist of your raised arm to get a feel for the strength. This is not a contest; this is simply the person trying to get an awareness of the level of resistance.

Continue to test by making a true statement about yourself. Raise your arm and test for strength. Then make an untrue statement about yourself and test for strength. The resistance should be noticeably less. There are many reasons for why this may not work. If you cannot have consistent, accurate test results, then abandon this method until you are with someone who has experience and can help you identify the issues. After successfully testing for compatibility, read and test yourself for each of the statements on the Personal Success Inventory. Then, add whatever statements you desire to explore.

CHAPTER 18

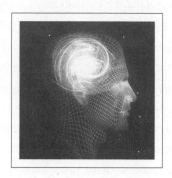

CAPTURING INSPIRATION

The creative man notices what others take for granted.

S OMETIMES IT SEEMS THAT the one thing separating the wage earner from the entrepreneurial creator of wealth is just one great idea! How many times have we seen a new product or service that made millions only to bemoan, "Why didn't I think of that?" The reason we ask ourselves this question is because so often the great idea solved a problem that was common to us all. It was something any of us could have figured out. But we didn't! Someone else acted upon the obvious and changed his or her financial world!

Why do some people seem to get great ideas and others don't? Is it a question of intelligence? No! Is it education? Not necessarily! Well then, what is the difference? Sadly no one really knows the exact answer to that. Sometimes it comes to those who are desperate. Sometimes it comes to those who have already amassed fortunes. Occasionally it comes to those who are down to the last moment before total destruction. It even comes to those who don't have a single need in their life. It's called inspiration!

WHEN AND WHO?

Inspiration is that flash of an idea, the sudden rush of understanding, that seems to come from nowhere only to find a perfect home in our mind. It is like the perfect marriage of time, circumstances and opportunity! Inspiration turns thousands of failed experiments into a light bulb that changes almost everything about the industrial world; a telephone that will connect people all over the world through instant personal communication; or a recipe from an elderly restaurateur that introduces what will become a world-famous chicken recipe. There are thousands of rags-to-riches stories that all revolve around one great idea!

Sometimes inspiration comes after years of trying and failing. Occasionally it occurs as the initial spark that launches thousands of experiments and as often as not it comes as the last play of the game, when tragedy seems inevitable. It's like the story of the man who invested all he had in cranberries. There was a definite market need. The problem, however, came at harvest. There was no financially effective way to harvest the cranberries.

According to the story, he was down to a single load of cranberries, on his way to sell the few he had harvested and face financial ruin. On his way to market his truck overturned and spilled the only profit he would make from his labors. Unexpectedly, the cranberries fell into a ditch filled with water and he noticed they floated. Like a lightning strike his answer came: flood the fields and the cranberries will float. He solved his harvesting problem and turned failure into success.

Then there is the story of a man who was doing business at a local store and took note of a promotional program they were offering. He saw the validity of the promotion, but he also immediately recognized how limited they were in their ability to take it to a larger market. Having great computer and marketing skills, he was able to take a very simple idea that worked on a very limited scale, recreate and expand it, and turn it into a multimillion-dollar marketing company.

There is little accounting for when inspiration will come. But there are some factors that tell us *who* inspiration will come to. Although it is impossible to make inspiration come, we can facilitate it so that we create the most likely opportunity for it to come to us. Attitude, more than anything, may determine who will experience inspiration. There is an attitude that expects and searches for opportunity and that somehow attracts inspiration. It is a peaceful optimism coupled with a "can do" mindset.

Attitude, more than anything, may determine who will experience inspiration.

One of the most familiar teachings of Jesus is *"Seek, and ye shall find."*[1] In the original language it actually says seek and keep on seeking and you will find! This is not the person who casually looks and then gives up. Neither is it the person who pessimistically looks with no hope of an answer. This is the person who believes there is a solution, an idea or an opportunity. These people believe they can do what needs to be done or at least learn what needs to be done to meet the need. They believe that their desire coupled with their persistent looking will be rewarded with the opportunity they desire and pursue.

Inspiration is an issue of the heart; conniving and scheming are the mental imposters of inspiration. In fact, conniving will block true inspiration. The person who finds inspiration is not the person who is searching in desperation, willing to violate ethics and use people. Inspiration comes to people of peace. I have heard it said that most great ideas came to people while they were relaxed, with their feet elevated, doing nothing and striving for nothing. Maybe the reason so many ideas come at the last minute is because that is when we give up. Then in a less "pushy" mentality we are able to receive what our heart has been trying to tell us all along.

The truth is all of us have received enough inspiration to solve most if not all of our problems and make us all wealthy. For the most part our issue isn't receiving inspiration; it is capturing and acting upon inspiration.

All of us have received enough inspiration to solve most if not all of our problems and make us all wealthy.

The word *inspiration* comes from the words *in spirit*. In other words, there was a time when inspiration was linked to God Himself, when to be inspired was to be in the Spirit. It was Divine! It is also interesting to note that there are nine Greek words that are all translated as sin. Sin, contrary to popular religious thinking, isn't so much about what we do wrong as much as it is missing what we could be, do or have. God is always attempting to inspire us to a quality of life that is better than anything we have ever imagined! Sin is when we don't grab the inspiration and enjoy the quality of life God is offering!

One of the nine Greek words translated as sin (missing the mark of what we could be, have or do) means "to hear amiss."[2] To hear amiss could mean many things, but as much as anything to hear amiss could be to hear and lose what we hear before we can actualize it. Most of us get inspiration, but we never realize what it actually could mean in our life because we do nothing to capture and activate it in our lives.

HOW TO KEEP OR LOSE INSPIRATION

Another great lesson in how the mind works was given by Jesus in what most people call the parable of the sower.[3] In this parable a messenger spreads the message. There are four types of environments that symbolize people's reactions to what they hear. The key question in this parable is what determines who will hear, hold on to and produce fruit—results—in response to what they hear.

In metaphoric terms Jesus explains exactly how the mind works. When we hear any opportunity or inspiration in an instant our subconscious mind runs that inspiration through a filter called "the critical conscience." In the critical conscience that inspiration is compared to everything we have ever done, experienced and believed about ourselves. Based on our previous life experience, we subconsciously determine if we

will accept or reject that inspiration. Some immediately and often unconsciously reject ideas before they ever enter the arena of conscious thought.
Others hold on to the inspiration until they run into rejection or hardship.
Then they let it go. But when the seed goes into good ground, it takes root,
grows and bears fruit!

Most inspiration is lost before we ever face rejection or hardship. It
is lost by failing to implement the one key factor for capturing inspiration.
Remember, inspiration is not just an idea. It is an emotionally charged
idea. It is not just a thought about what could be done. It is a thought
about what *I* could do! It is an idea that carries the emotional motivation
to take action. It is an idea that is experienced as real.

But most of these ideas are lost. Jesus gave us insight into the one
key for capturing inspiration. *The degree of thought and study you give to
what you hear determines the degree of life that will come back to you.* Thought,
study, pondering and meditation are ways to personalize what we hear.
We know that a person must take ownership of or in some way begin to
implement inspiration. If not, it will only remain with us for a maximum
of 12 hours.

When inspiration is gone we may remember the information, but we lose the emotion. It
doesn't feel the same. It doesn't move us like it
did when it first came to us. In fact, we may even
question ourselves, "What did I think was so
great about this?" It no longer moves us to action.
We lose the sense of ourselves doing something
great with what we hear.

The very first thing that will come to steal
inspiration from us is self-accusation. We talk
ourselves out of inspiration by rehearsing all the
reasons we can't do it. Then, as we mentioned
earlier, if we make it past self-accusation we face

*We must take
ownership
of or in some
way begin to
implement
inspiration. If
not, it will only
remain with us
for a maximum
of 12 hours.*

the other distractions that Jesus mentioned in His parable. If we don't over-spiritualize the meaning, we can easily see the distractions that tend to move us away from inspiration.

The only way to capture inspiration is to think, ponder, study and meditate on it.

The only way to capture inspiration is to think, ponder, study and meditate on it. That's what it means to "be careful"[4] about what you hear. If we respond to inspiration by thinking about it—what it would look like, how we could do it—and see ourselves putting it into practice, then we are personalizing it, taking ownership of it and conceptualizing it. We are making it ours! These actions allow the inspiration to grow in the soil of our heart and bear the fruit of a realized dream!

When you get an idea, immediately write it down. As someone has said, "The most faded ink is better than the clearest memory." Just the act of writing affects our memory. Then take a few minutes and write every creative thought that comes to you concerning your inspiration. Don't stop writing until the ideas stop flowing. With the advent of PDAs I keep my personal inspiration on my phone notepad. That way every time I have a thought I can add to the list of ideas. More than once I have outlined an entire book in less than ten minutes. I have written complete songs in 20 minutes. But I have probably lost more ideas than I ever captured. I learned the costly way what it means to hear amiss. Now I treasure all inspiration and treat it as the very breath of God!

When a heart is looking for opportunity but not pushing, when it is open to creativity but not forcing, when we get in that paradox of ready to run but in complete rest, it is amazing what we will hear bubble up from our heart. Inspiration will deliver that next brilliant idea or the occasional complete plan that seems to come from nowhere yet consumes our every sensibility. It can bring that next great breakthrough that dramatically changes our life, and sometimes the entire world.

Inspiration has been the key to the greatest discoveries in our world. Great minds throughout history like Einstein, Ford and others seemed to be masters at capturing inspiration. The one thing they all realized is that you have to be in a relaxed state for inspiration to come. You can't make it happen; you can only facilitate the environment that calls it forth. Whether you are capable of deep meditation or you have mastered the art of finding that neutral place of rest, you can experience incredible inspiration.

Inspiration has been the key to the greatest discoveries in our world.

In Heart Physics® the first thing we teach people is how to relax the physical body. Besides all the obvious health benefits, relaxing the body is a prerequisite to connecting with the heart and breaking free of the controlling frantic delusions of the mind. In the absence of the mind's limiting control we learn to allow the heart to referee, and we will then know how to use our intellectual mind but keep it under the guidance of a peaceful heart.

Remember, God speaks in your heart through intuitive inspiration. He knows everything. He knows how to solve every problem, and He is always speaking to you! By facilitating the voice of your heart you are facilitating the voice of the Creator of all things, the ultimate model of success. He will lead you into the success that is perfect for your life!

CHAPTER 19

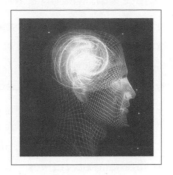

CREATING A NEW NORMAL

That which is embraced by your mind's eye becomes more real than your circumstances!

W E ALL HAVE OUR own individual sense of normal. It is the self-imposed standard we have come to accept. It provides the bar we will raise as our standard and the limitation of how far we can go. Our normal is the place within the established boundaries of the heart, which feels familiar and therefore creates the illusion of safety! The truth is, however, normal may not be safe at all. It may be the least safe of all our options. But, because we tend to view the unknown as threatening, we will stubbornly dig in our heels and opt for the familiar and often deceptive feelings of sameness, all the while withdrawing from the multitude of potential opportunities.

Every day we see the *familiar* trap people into destructive situations. As an outsider it makes no sense to us at all. We objectively recognize the danger, but to the person trapped inside the choice of sameness or uncertainty, the view is slanted by the subjectivity of familiarity! How often have we seen someone refuse to leave an abusive marriage? Her life may actually be in danger. But she stays. It is not safe but it is familiar, which is often less threatening than the unknown. Likewise, the opportunity for advancement is not always met with welcome arms.

In one eye-opening case, an individual who wanted to break the bounds of his current income reluctantly began the use of a simple heart exercise for moving his financial boundaries. As it turns out, he had topped out with his present company. There was no opportunity for advancement. Yet, he had never considered changing jobs. After a few weeks of daily Heart exercises, he lost his job. At first it seemed like everything was working against his efforts. In the end, not only did he find a new job, but it actually exceeded his financial objectives. The obvious that had been unseen before the turn of events was that he would have had to change jobs to advance. This was beyond his comfort zone. Yet, the daily Heart exercises took him to a place he had not only been unwilling to go to, but also had been unable to see!

Only by expanding the boundaries of his heart could he face the incredible challenges of such dramatic change. But he had seen firsthand the effectiveness of expanding his boundaries. When faced with another need for financial growth it was suggested that he repeat the Heart exercise. To the surprise of his coach he adamantly refused. He was unwilling to face that much uncertainty even though he believed the experiment would work a second time. That which was familiar but kept him in lack was chosen over that which was proven but would require change.

WHAT IS "NORMAL"?

The mind seeks to keep one within the bounds of the known. It will convince us to stay out of love, keep a bad job or never expect happiness… and it will all make sense! The mind can come up with such corrupted logic, and we fall for it. If we took the time to get into the place of peace, listen to and follow our heart, we would peacefully remove ourselves from all threatening situations while maintaining our sense of dignity and worth. Every day people choose to stay in jobs that really don't meet their needs, put up with abusive bosses or work in deplorable situations all because it is familiar (normal).

Our heart seeks to preserve our self-worth. People who have a healthy self-worth and listen to their heart will always have healthy boundaries. They think too well of themselves to tolerate denigration and belittlement. They realize the need to guard their heart. If we allow anyone to minimize our value, we reduce the scope of our boundaries. Our life, purpose and courage become smaller and smaller as we accept the violation of our boundaries and the minimizing of our dignity!

Our "normal," whether we like it or not, is something that we have accepted.

Our "normal," whether we like it or not, is something we have accepted. By default, to accept is to choose. As far as the heart knows we have chosen everything that is in our life simply because we accepted it. When it becomes accepted the heart resists giving it up because we have, after all, chosen it as the life we want.

When circumstances occur that cause us to feel stress we have the opportunity to act, solve the problem and remove the stress. If we do nothing, then in a short time that which caused us stress in the beginning becomes unnoticed. The mind causes us to stop noticing it as a way to reduce some level of conscious stress. Sadly, we think that which is unnoticed is gone, but nothing is farther from the truth. Out of sight may be out of mind, but out of mind does not mean it is out of influence. Unresolved issues are always at work on an "other than conscious" level.

Once something is ignored, it is considered to be accepted or chosen. Once it is accepted we adjust or rearrange our life so we can function with the problem. I use the example of a twig growing up through your living room floor. At first it is an irritation, possibly an embarrassment. Although you notice you do nothing about it. So it keeps growing. It has been accepted (tolerated). Once it gets big enough you start rearranging your furniture so you can be comfortable with its presence. It even becomes a conversation piece. It has gone past being accepted; it is now part of your identity. Once something is factored into your identity it is needed to feel normal. At this point you would resist any attempt to remove the tree that started out as such an annoyance!

The physical body works the same way. If you were to hurt one of the many muscles in your foot, all the rest of the body would have to compensate so you could walk with minimal pain. Your ankle, knee, hip and spine all would have to make minor adjustments so you can still walk on that foot. These adjustments will eventually become *the way you walk*. It is part of your normal. Each of the adjustments could evolve into a disease of its own. No matter how much you treated your knee, hip or spine, the problem would never completely go away until the foot injury was resolved.

> *By the time an issue becomes needed, it is familiar and we will resist its removal. We don't know how to be normal without it!*

Once we have left any issue unresolved we begin to make the mental, emotional or financial adjustments wherein we build our life and logic around the problem. Once we have made all these adjustments the problem becomes part of our identity. It is who we are! It is our normal! We have designed our life to function with the problem. The thing that was first seen as an irritation, a negative or even an obstacle is now needed to preserve our sense of self. By the time an issue becomes needed, it is familiar. Now that it is familiar we will resist its removal. We don't know how to be normal without it!

Some studies indicate that many children in abusive homes, when given the opportunity to leave, will choose to stay. Why, you have to ask, would any child stay in an abusive home? It is familiar! It is less threatening than the unknown. It is their sense of normal. As a result of accepting this normal, their heart has been affected. Their sense of self has been reduced and their boundaries moved inward. This is exactly what happens to us financially or relationally. The limits we accept define our sense of self and establish our boundaries. We keep choosing jobs, spouses and friends who will keep us within the boundaries of our normal. Even our health and energy will succumb to the heart's attempts to keep us in our sense of normal!

DECEPTIONS OF THE MIND

The mind will play all manner of tricks to keep us accepting its boundaries of familiarity. One of the common responses to irritations is to complain. Complaining is a deceptive delusion wherein we appear to be doing something about the problem. Complaining is usually a form of passive aggressive behavior. As passives we never actually address the problem in a proactive, productive manner. But complaining gives the illusion that we are actually doing something about the problem. Complaining is a way to appear to resist the problem while actually accepting it!

Complaining is a deceptive delusion wherein we appear to be doing something about the problem.

Financial limitations are very often a source of complaints. But complaining does nothing to create a new sense of normal. In fact, complaining about a problem actually magnifies it and makes us more aware of the sense of normal that we are accepting. Complaining moves a problem from the realm of resolvable to impossible. It makes the problem appear more ominous than it is. It is a downward cycle of enlarging the problem while deflating hope, leaving no avenue of reprieve but more complaining!

Complaining is actually a form of meditation. In meditation we think about something until we produce the associated emotions, which reinforces it as real or absolute—that is, our normal! Complaining is one of the many ways we revisit the past or the present and magnify a problem until it gets larger in our experience than it was. Rethinking and complaining reinforces the idea that "this" is our normal. This is our plight in life.

Resisting our circumstances often creates more stress and reinforces the fatalistic sense of normal. The modern notion of resistance is to attack the problem. Attacking the problem is another of the many deceptive

> *The greatest and only healthy form of resisting internal circumstances is to align ourselves with the solution.*

reactions that actually focuses our attention on and magnifies the problem beyond solution. The greatest and only healthy form of resisting internal circumstances is to align ourselves with the solution. We clearly see the problem, but do we clearly see the solution? The moment we focus on the solution we are no longer aligned with the problem. But only by creating a desirable solution can we resist our problem while magnifying the answer!

MEDITATE A NEW NORMAL

The easiest way to establish a new normal is to preview the life you chose—meditation! Meditation is a biblical and psychological process whereby we make that which is unseen, seen. It is a way of seeing that which exists potentially but is not yet a concrete reality. The word *meditate* has many meanings according to what language is spoken. In Hebrew it can mean to mutter over and over again, to ponder, to complain, to frame or to converse with one's self.[1] It is an inclusive process wherein we rehearse a matter until it becomes real. It is a way to create familiarity while aligning ourselves with the life we want, more than the life we have!

> *We make the future real by first making it normal in our thoughts and dreams.*

We all meditate! In fact, our tomorrow is the emotional picture we paint on the canvas of our mind today. We make the future real by first making it normal in our thoughts and dreams. In journeying beyond our current boundaries of success we need to think about it, read books about those who have made the journey, talk about it, ponder it and in every possible way make it not only real but familiar.

In learning to create a new normal many people employ a disciplined approach to meditation. Others simply think, study, talk and ponder. It really doesn't matter how you do it as long as you do something that engages the imagination and creates strong, positive emotions. In fact, the greatest way to bring about the most rapid change with the least amount of stress is to employ as many different methods as you have available. Formal meditation to daydreaming—it is all beneficial.

Before I had ever made more than a million dollars in a year, I would do things like write large checks (from old closed accounts and I immediately destroyed them) to causes I wanted to support for thousands of dollars. That was something I had never done. It was not a part of my normal. In fact, it was just the opposite of my normal. But I wanted to know what it felt like. After spending time in meditation, while still in the emotional rush of a new reality, I would write out these checks. Little did I know that by writing in longhand, I was actually implementing another powerful tool in my arsenal for creating a new future!

As it turns out, writing in longhand is part of a continuum whereby what is in the subconscious is expressed through your handwriting. Thus, you have the science of handwriting analysis. As a continuum it not only sends signals from the mind to the hand that express your inner feelings, it also sends signals from your hand to your subconscious. Handwriting while still in a meditative state bypasses the conscious mind and influences the inner man by the words you write.

The real trick to creating a new normal without creating stress lies in our ability and willingness to lead with our heart and not our mind. According to some research it seems that making positive affirmations, for many people, creates more stress. Based on what we know about stress, this would push the thing hoped for further away. It would not make it more real; it would make it unreal and undesirable.

In the 1970s and 80s the Christian world was overrun with the teachings of positive confession. At the same time the self-development world paralleled the Christian with positive affirmations. Although there are many potentially healthy benefits associated with this approach, for many it proved to be a road to frustration and disillusionment. The brain could easily view these positive statements as a journey into the unknown, which would be interpreted as a threat, resulting in stress. If the heart did not really believe the things being acknowledged were factual, then our conscience would view them as lies, again leading to an outcome of stress not peace.

The concept of confession from a biblical viewpoint comes from the Greek word which means "to say the same thing."[2] Simply saying something does not equate confession. The idea behind a confession is, "It must be true!" The same philosophy applies for positive affirmations. There must be a basis for an affirmation to be true or it could have a negative consequence. Ideally, it must be true in at least two other arenas before we can speak it as a confession. It must be true based on the Word of God, and it must be true in our heart. Then and only then can we speak that which is unseen with the confidence that it is true. The same holds true for the person seeking to make a positive affirmation. There must be some basis for believing the affirmation is true or it could create the stress associated with lying.

To make a confession/affirmation true it must first be a realty we have chosen. We must choose the desired outcome. The promises of God give us a spiritual basis to speak the unseen into existence. But then comes the personal and most challenging part. We must see/perceive it as real in our own heart. The imagination is the precognitive capacity of man. By imagining something so clearly that it becomes real and familiar to

> *The imagination is the precognitive capacity of man.*

us, it is no longer viewed as a threat. Using the imagination to make something real is a form of meditation. Whether we do it for a few minutes throughout the day or whether we set aside lengthy periods of time, it is all meditation.

Create images and pictures of you living and experiencing the quality of life you desire. Don't be random…be specific. See yourself doing things with your newfound wealth that will bring you great pleasure and fulfillment. Creating pleasure is key! The more you can see yourself living a certain lifestyle, paying bills, giving to causes, driving a better car, providing for your children or whatever motivates you, the sooner you will have a new sense of normal. But the absolute keys to making meditation work are: It must be what you have chosen. You must see yourself doing the things you desire to do. You must experience massive amounts of pleasure while previewing your new life. You must do it until the desire becomes a present tense reality. And finally, you must get in the place of peace and discover what actions you must take to make this journey!

CHAPTER 20

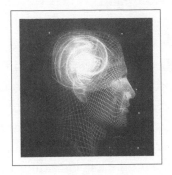

RESETTING YOUR THERMOSTAT

Success requires the same effort as failure and is not nearly as painful!

A S WE HAVE PREVIOUSLY discussed the heart is like a thermostat. Once it is set it may allow your life to rise a few degrees above the normal you have chosen and it may allow your life to sink a few degrees beneath your sense of normal, but it will always kick in to bring your life back to your setting for normal!

When your sense of self was established by default, this "coming back to normal" is an egregious cycle from which there seems no escape. But when your sense of self is consciously chosen this cycle is like the function of the parasympathetic nervous system. They both work for you with no conscious effort on your part! Thus the promise of Heart Physics®: positive, permanent, painless, effortless change!

EFFORTLESS CHANGE

Effortless change is impossible when it is sought through behavior modification. You may change the behavior, but inwardly it always requires effort. Then on a day that you are too tired or too frustrated to put forth the effort you find yourself rebounding into the old destructive behaviors. It is this continual trying and failing that finally persuades your heart that change is just too hard. When you believe change is just too hard the only remaining solution is to justify the very behavior that is robbing your finances and life!

There will always be some effort involved in change. The question is, will it be the wasted effort of trying to control your behavior or the fruitful effort of changing your beliefs? The New Testament puts forth an interesting paradox: *"Labor to enter into rest."*[1] At a casual glance this seems like a contradictory concept. If you're laboring, then you're not resting. So it becomes obvious that the labor is the process of persuading your heart to believe. Once a new belief is installed, the laboring is over. From that point on you're on automatic pilot. The change is effortless; installing the belief was the place of effort!

If you now have success written on your heart, then just as surely as your heart effortlessly led you into destructive financial decisions in the past, it will now lead you down a path of success in the future. And that success will require no more conscious effort than it had previously taken to fail! Success is not hard; failing is hard…it's really hard! Both success and failure require the same effort. It is not even the believing that is hard. The only thing that is hard is trying to change your behavior without changing your beliefs!

When seeking success we are usually impatiently attempting to pack massive amounts of change into a short period of time. We hear the clock ticking. We feel the pain of the circumstances created by years of destructive beliefs. Because we often wait until the pain forces us to deal with our beliefs, we are daily struggling against circumstances and emotions. This makes change seem hard. But the reality is, we *will* overcome years of destructive behavior in a very short time. The road to recovery is always shorter than the road to destruction. We are wired to heal and rebound!

THE SECRET TO QUICK CHANGE

One of the laws of physics tells us that in order for the motion of an object to change, a force must act upon it. Obviously the greater the mass and intensity of the object acting on the other, the greater and quicker the change! The greater the emotion you create about the new belief you desire to install, the quicker and more dramatic the change!

Every belief of the heart is the result of information plus emotion. At some time of strong emotions we either thought something or heard something. The combination of those two factors, if strong enough or persistent enough, can create a deep heart belief.

> *Every belief of the heart is the result of information plus emotion.*
>
> ❧

However, just as it took these two components emotion and information to install an old destructive belief, so it will take these two components to uninstall that old belief and install a new one. The difference is we choose the belief and we create the type of emotion we want associated with that belief!

In the hierarchy of behavior, one of our core motivating factors is the perception of pain and pleasure. Pain and pleasure are an outgrowth of a deeper motivator: love and fear. The more pleasure or positive emotions we can attach to the belief we desire to install, the quicker, easier and deeper it is incorporated into our sense of self! Likewise, the more pain we associate with the old belief, the quicker and easier it is uninstalled. The key is to connect massive amounts of pleasure to the belief you choose and massive amounts of pain to the one you reject.

In the Creating Wealth Heart Physics® program we design exercises to help you identify old limiting beliefs and attach to them the pain they deserve. We also teach you how to incorporate new, positive, healthy beliefs by attaching massive amounts of pleasure to them. Sometimes in less than 30 minutes people identify and uninstall old beliefs and then install a new, powerful life-changing financial belief. Just imagine bringing an end to a lifetime struggle in such little time.

We have had people who had gone through years of extensive therapy and attended a dozen financial self-help workshops with no change. The great thing is that all the information that was learned is not wasted.

When your heart beliefs change, every motivation and financial key you have ever learned starts working for you! None of your other efforts are a waste when your heart aligns with healthy financial beliefs!

THE PROCESS OF CHANGE

All change starts with desire or frustration. Either the expectation of pleasure or the dread of more pain is always the motivator! The expectation of pleasure can be the result of inspiration, a motivational seminar, a good book or a teaching program. The pain usually comes from failed goals, financial pressure and lost dreams.

Desire then inspires a decision. A decision is not a decision to try; it is a decision to do! Trying is another resistance game of the mind. An absolute decision is one where you cut off all other options. You make no emotional room for failure. As an ancient proverb says, "When the student is ready the teacher appears." You are probably reading this book because you got ready and your heart brought you the tools! That's just the way it works.

A decision is not a decision to try; it is a decision to do!

The very first active step of application would be to identify the limiting belief, behavior or emotion. Use the exercises provided in Chapter 17. If you are uncomfortable at performing those exercises, then you can use the "Limiting Beliefs" meditation. It is a powerful exercise. In fact, I have used this exercise to help more people resolve more problems than any other single exercise I have ever developed.

Attempting to move forward without dealing with the limiting beliefs is like trying to swim while carrying a bunch of suitcases. The suitcases represent the emotional baggage we are carrying that is prohibiting our ability to do something that would otherwise be quite easy. Get rid of the baggage and you'll find yourself easily swimming toward your goals and dreams.

The next exercise we teach in the Creating Wealth Heart Physics® program is called "painting a new life picture." This exercise is too extensive to be explained in this space. But you can begin applying a small part of it. Each night about 15-20 minutes before going to sleep write two or three positive, personal and present tense affirmations about your current financial goal. This is not a time to deal with several different subjects. This is the time to focus on one financial goal. Be sure to write these affirmations in longhand and do them every night, just before going to sleep.

Then when you awake in the morning you will be in a deep meditative state for about three minutes. Sit up on the side of the bed and reaffirm those affirmations. If you don't sit up, then you will probably go back to sleep. If you have taken our Essential Heart Physics® program, you can count yourself down to your Heart Zone before making the affirmations.

Then while in that deep state, create a mental movie of your doing something that represents the fulfillment of that goal. See or imagine yourself as clearly as you possibly can. Maybe you will imagine yourself paying off a debt or moving into a new house. You have to choose the goal that creates the most emotional momentum for you. The key thing is not just seeing the goal; the key thing is noticing what you feel. Allow yourself to experience this as a present tense reality. Give thanks for the goal being reached; honor God in the process. Acknowledge that you trust Him to provide wisdom in your heart. Acknowledge that you have chosen this reality and when you open your eyes this will be the reality that will guide your life. Count yourself up from 1-5 and enjoy the day.

The key thing is not just seeing the goal; the key thing is noticing what you feel.

❧

Then throughout the day do several mini-meditations, or mini-meds. Mini-meds are those times where you take just 30 to 45 seconds and recreate the mental movie that represents you reaching your financial goals. Take just enough time to see them and feel the emotions. Mini-meds are incredible at changing the way you think throughout the day.

A multi-modality approach is always the best. Using several different types of heart tools at different times of the day will affect different aspects of your thinking processes and ensure a more absolute outcome.

CHAPTER 21

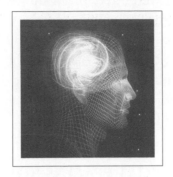

FOLLOWING THE WAY OF PEACE

Peace is the compass that leads us down the paths we can trust!

IN WORKING CLOSELY WITH people who have made bad financial decisions, I have seen the devastation such decisions can bring to a family. I have seen dreams lost and destinies postponed because people made decisions they thought were good! In those painful moments of regret I've heard it said more times than I can count, "I don't understand; I really felt good about this!" This is the confused cry of people who have made bad decisions only to discover they had been duped by their own emotions. There are many emotions and attitudes we easily confuse with peace: excitement, optimism and motivation, to name a few. Even the false peace of greed and lust can come when we feel we have gotten what we wanted.

After years of working as a health care provider, counselor and life coach I have discovered that very few people enjoy a very consistent level of peace. In fact peace is so foreign that many not only fail to recognize it, but they also wouldn't know it if it visited them. In my clinic I have often given people treatments designed to bring them to a place of physiological peace prior to attempting to resolve the major health issue. I knew unless I relieved stress all efforts at restoring health would be temporary at best.

Many times my patients would come in the next day and I would ask them how their evening went. Very often they would complain of headaches or other discomforts. Upon close examination I would discover that as the feelings of peace came on them, it was so foreign they would resist it. Peace was so alien to them that they thought they were slipping into sleep or fatigue. They would drink caffeine or do any number of things to resist this unknown feeling! Usually before I could ever get them well, I had to first get them acquainted with peace.

WHAT PEACE IS NOT

In the book *The Healing Code* Dr. Alex Loyd and Ben Johnson point out some startling discoveries. They report that most people are in physiological stress but have no awareness of it. They describe having a room with a hundred people. They would ask how many felt stressed. For their example they would say if 50 percent indicated they didn't feel stress and 50 percent indicated they did, they would test the 50 percent who said they did not feel stress. Drs. Loyd and Johnson found that about 95 percent of those who said they did not feel stress would actually test positive for stress.[1] People have become so accustomed to living in physiological and emotional stress that the closest thing they have to peace is a little less stress.

People have become so accustomed to living in physiological and emotional stress that the closest thing they have to peace is a little less stress.

As documented by research at The HeartMath Institute as well as at a number of other reputable sources, when people reach a place of stress or anxiety their mind isolates itself from the information coded in the heart waves. In other words, they stop hearing the voice of the heart! The heart, which is supposed to be the guiding factor for life, is so alienated from our conscious experience that we either seldom hear it or fail to discern the imposters of the mind!

We have become so out of touch with our heart and so dominated by our intellectual mind and corrupt concepts that we accept the mind's substitutes for the heart's peace. The mind substitutes familiarity for peace. Being right is often confused with peace. Sometimes we make bad decisions to get relief. Relief is often as close to peace as we know how to relate! As good as it may be to have these feelings, they cannot help guide our life into the kind of life choices we need.

The mind is great for gathering facts. But, when used for decision making, it is primarily driven by the ego, the self. As such it leads us to decisions for which we can take credit. It limits the available options to our intellectual knowledge or our life's experiences. Furthermore, in a world that has become increasingly anti-God there is no room for the wisdom of a Creator in whom we do not believe! Even Christianity has become a heartless religion instead of a heart connection with our Creator! We are a culture that does not know how to live out of our heart.

We are a culture that does not know how to live out of our heart.

HEART PEACE

God always speaks to our heart. Even when our heart is limited to a negative self-concept God is always breathing inspiration into the heart. It doesn't even matter if we do not believe in God. He believes in us and He is showing His love to us by giving ideas that are bigger than our mind could ever conceive. And amazingly He will then lead us down the path to live those dreams in a way that expands our hearts in the journey. In the end, if we recognize the wisdom that comes from beyond ourselves, we can't help but trust and follow this God of peace. But the path God will lead us in will always be the path of peace. That's where we run into our conflict. Don't think that because you're a Christian you are immune to this issue. Believers are just as conflicted about the way of peace as non-believers.

One of the greatest indictments in the Bible against mankind says, *"The way of peace they have not known."*[2] The long list of ramifications resulting from this essential flaw is shocking. Our modern society is based on force. People get what they want by using physical, emotional or financial force. Force is always met with resistance on some level. Ironically, force doesn't create stress just for the abused; it also creates stress for the abuser. We were not wired to function from the place of force. It is a diabolical strategy based on the flawed logic of self-centeredness: I win, you lose! Whereas love works from the attitude that says: As much as it lies within me, we will both win! The stress created by moving in force often makes it impossible for either party to recognize the voice of his or her heart. Chaos is inevitable!

> ## *The heart is my deepest beliefs about me.*

The heart is the seat of understanding—not intellectual understanding but understanding about who I am and what I will *really* do. The heart is my deepest beliefs about me. All beliefs of the heart are understood only in light of how they affect my sense of self. There are things I can do, but the truth is I probably won't do them, at least not for long! Many of my failures came from the flawed ego-based mentality that says, "I should be able to do this!" Or, by comparing myself to others, "If he can do this, I know I can." My ego or naivety would move me into a commitment that my heart knew I would not finish. But I wasn't listening to my heart. I was listening to my mind and failing to recognize the imposters of peace that my mind offers.

I often receive calls and emails from people who want me to advise them on investments or business opportunities. They start out asking the wrong question, "Do you think this is a good deal?" The answer to that question is relative to what you believe about yourself in your heart. No deal is right for everyone. So often people think I'm holding out on them when I decline to offer the advice they seek. You see, not every deal is a good deal. It may be good for someone but that doesn't mean it is good for you. If I can help you get in touch with your heart, then you will be able to recognize if it is the right deal for you!

One day while walking through my neighborhood, I noticed a house for sale. I had wanted to bring up the property values in the old neighborhood. I thought this might be a good place to start. I felt peace. I called the man who had the house and discovered he had four houses in the neighborhood that he was willing to sell. I didn't have any money for a down payment but I followed the wisdom of my heart…I listened; I had a sense about these houses. So I negotiated owner finances at a great price for all four.

I left the office and before the afternoon was over I negotiated the sale of one house with a large enough down payment to me, to pay the down payment for all four. Within weeks they were all sold with commitments from each of the buyers to totally renovate them. That one transaction resulted in 14 houses being bought, remodeled and sold. The property values in my neighborhood went up more than 600 percent in just a few years. I put young families into great houses thousands of dollars below the appraised value. They all had equity in their homes, I made a great profit and the neighborhood was forever changed!

I don't have a real estate seminar telling you how to buy property with no money. I can't tell you how to buy houses and flip them. But I can tell you that I followed my own heart just like you can follow your own heart. But there must be enough acquaintance with your heart that you can discern the difference between the voice of your mind and the voice of your heart.

PEACE IS A STATE OF BEING

Our first misunderstanding about peace is simply this: Peace is not a goal; it is a state…a state of being. If peace is approached as a goal it becomes another variable based on external factors over which we must gain control. It puts us back in the force mode. If we force everything and everyone around us to be and do what we want, then we have *false* peace.

This external approach creates more stress and conflict. At best we may gain the momentary substitute of relief in lieu of peace, in those brief moments that everything goes right! But eventually people and circumstances move beyond our control and there is no peace!

Peace is not a goal; it is a state of being.

Peace is a state of being. It is internal. It is how we relate to the world because of how we relate to ourselves. When we are at peace with God and at peace with ourselves, we abide in a habitual state of peace that is completely independent of external factors. In this state of peace we quickly recognize the subtle intuitive *ripples* that we feel when that which we intend is incongruent with whom we are.

The New Testament gives incredible insight into following the way of peace. It says, *"Let the peace of God rule in your hearts!"*[3] This word for peace means to arbitrate, rule or umpire.[4] In baseball the umpire is the one who determines if the ball is safe or foul! Our heart can give us wisdom that is beyond our intelligence. Our heart knows if the situation is safe for who we are and how we function! Remember, holistic success is about effectively doing that which is congruent with who we are and the lives we have chosen to live. Our heart leads us into a tailor-made success. It might not fit anyone else but it is perfect for us!

The number one cause of internal confusion is when a decision has been made that violates your internal wisdom.

When making decisions, get physically relaxed. You can't relax emotionally while physically tense or stressed. If you have something you do that calms you, whether prayer, music meditation or breathing exercises, utilize them. Surrender all personal preferences. The number one cause of internal confusion is when a decision has been made that violates your internal wisdom. Confusion becomes the emotional default to justify pursuing the predetermined path and disregard the voice of your heart.

When in a place of complete relaxation, with no preferences, breathe deeply and slowly. You may even do about 3-10 breaths in through your nose, deep into your belly and out slowly through slightly parted lips. This is an amazingly simple yet effective way to relax. In that relaxed state don't analyze, just ask: Do I really feel peace about this decision? Be specific about the decision. Then just wait and see how you feel. In the beginning it may be a little difficult, but the more peace becomes a way of life, the easier and quicker you will know. Then follow peace, even when it doesn't make sense.

I have lost millions of dollars by not following my heart and I have made millions by trusting my heart. After any decision I am always brutally honest with myself. When I get it wrong I want to know what types of emotions, feelings and thoughts were really driving my decisions. Moreover, when I get it right I want to know what was occurring internally. I have learned so much about me by taking inventory after each failure and each success. No classroom could have taught me these invaluable life lessons.

If you can, get in a relaxed state or find a way to feel safe while reviewing any past decision. As you view that decision-making process from a safe place, you will notice the thoughts, feelings and motives that actually drove the decision. In future decisions you will recognize when those same factors are present. You will become internally aware and gain the capability of making decisions more in line with your own hearts belief.

SOME PRACTICAL TOOLS

In the Creating Wealth, Heart Physics® program we teach a number of tools that can be easily utilized to determine internal beliefs. As people become proficient utilizing these tools they become more acquainted with the underlying driving factors. In time they begin noticing the factors before they act, instead of after. Plus, we show you how to experience what it would be like to make decisions with values that are more consistent with who you are. When you can see yourself functioning in a different way, it becomes believable. When it becomes believable it is within your grasp.

When approaching a decision and seeking to follow the way of peace you can take a personal inventory that will help you maintain holistic success.

1. Is the decision I'm about to make going to create an outcome of peace or conflict?
2. Do I feel so desperate I feel like I must get this deal to work?
3. Have I sought help from someone qualified in this area?
4. Do I feel rushed or led?
5. Is this consistent with who I am as a person?
6. Does this reflect my values, ethics and morals?
7. Is my family supportive of this decision?
8. Does my family know how they will be affected?
9. Will I walk away from this if I lose my peace?
10. Am I being driven by any negative emotions?

The way of peace may be foreign in the beginning but in the end it is the safest, most enjoyable path one could ever walk. There are many paths in life; many lead to destruction, some lead to costly success, but only the path of pace leads to a success that is suited perfectly for you! Never abandon it and you will be rich in every area of your life!

CHAPTER 22

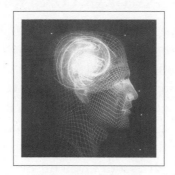

THE ULTIMATE CULTURAL CORRUPTION

We corrupt our leaders by allowing them to make our choices!

CULTURAL BELIEFS ARE AMONG the most powerful. They are also the hardest to recognize. Few people know the difference between the beliefs they have chosen and those that have been imposed on them by culture. Because cultural concepts are part of the ingrained view of the world by the people around us, it seems foolish to even question them. But possibly the most powerful dynamic of the accepted cultural view is the fact that we will be socially ostracized if we go against the collective view of the masses. Because of the power our culture has on affecting our belief, we must be vigilant to maintain an awareness of current trends of thought lest we accept them as our own and create an overpowering limiting belief!

The most formidable opponent to healthy heart beliefs about success and prosperity are being poured on us from each of the sources we were once most able to trust: the government, the school systems and the news media. When the voice of society becomes widespread and overwhelming it is assumed that the voice is true. When anything becomes a socially accepted norm everyone feels obliged to be in agreement.

THE UNSPOKEN CONSPIRACY

Please understand that I am not talking about a conspiracy. There are conspira*cies*! Powerful conspiracies! Don't fool yourself into thinking that many of the global businesses, organizations and governmental entities are not conspiracies on some level. However, it would not matter whether there were or were not spoken, agreed conspiracies. The greatest conspiracy is the unspoken conspiracy. The unspoken conspiracy grows from the greed and lust for power that works in the hearts of unregenerate men and women. It is the shared mindset of much of society.

The apostle Paul refers to it like this: *"The prince of the power of the air, the spirit who now works in the sons of disobedience."*[1] There is a system that is the way of the world. Those who do not have their hearts renewed by the Lord Jesus are under the influence of the prince of that system. Does this mean they are demon-possessed fanatics? No! It means that in a heart that is not ruled by love there is another system, another way of thought. You see, there is an unspoken agreement among those who do not value human life, do not value God and do not value integrity and morality. This unspoken conspiracy is a conspiracy of the heart that is followed by the majority of the world! The lust of this system is power and control; the way of this system is deceit, force and cruelty. The means to fulfill the objectives of this system are to control the resources—the wealth! Possibly more important than sharing the wealth is the strategic removing of resources from the control of the common man. When the common man has to come to the government/elite to get the resources, the borrower becomes servant to the lender. Free enterprise is a spiritual principle, even though it is often misused.

This unspoken conspiracy is a conspiracy of the heart that is followed by the majority of the world!

Over the past 50 years this unspoken conspiracy has developed a voice. This voice, although very subtle, has worked its way into our schools, our government and the media, and it has presented a faulty logic that is corrupting the essence of our nation and our Christianity. Since the development of a Department of Education and the incredible lobbying power of the NEA, education in America has plummeted. We no longer lead the world in education. Among comparable countries, cbsnews.com says, the United States rates ninth.[2] As with most things, once the government got involved, that which was working stopped working!

The decline of America's rank in education is not the worst factor. In the same article, entitled "U.S. Education Slips In Ranking," the writer refers to Barry McGaw, director of education for the Paris-based Organization for Cooperation and Development, as saying that "the United States remains atop the 'knowledge economy,' one that uses information to produce economic benefits. But, [McGaw] said, 'education's contribution to that economy is weakening, and you ought to be worrying.'"[3] In other words, education in America is not contributing to our economy.

How did our education system get to be so bad? Why is it that no one knows what to do? The problem isn't that no one knows what to do. The problem has nothing to do with education. This is not an education issue; this is a political issue. Reasonable parents and citizens think the debate is about education when in fact our government and the NEA are working a political agenda. Education is not as important as indoctrination.

Over at least the past 50 years there has been a slow, deliberate, planned effort to indoctrinate our children against God, human life, free enterprise, capitalism and even America. The history books have been rewritten to distort the values and motives of our founding fathers. The Constitution is not taught or valued. Evolution is taught as absolute fact even though many great scientific minds strongly disagree, and the godless science does not really support the theories. But there is a root

The one root that is being promoted in our schools is socialism!

to this tree. These are not random ideas that coincidentally emerged on the scene. The one root that is being promoted in our schools is socialism!

All of these seemingly non-connected anomalies have one common root: socialism!

IT'S ALL ABOUT SOCIALISM

Socialism is a philosophical idea that says it is giving power to the people, while in fact it facilitates the giving of total power to a few people who will not just make laws that control our behavior, but also will make laws that control what we are allowed to think. It paves the way for the one battle that has raged since the Garden of Eden, where man can finally rule this world independent of God!

Socialism has never worked. Yet our children are taught in school that it is a glowing success throughout history. Capitalism is portrayed as a greedy, power hungry system whereby the rich rule over the poor and turn them into slaves. The truth is, capitalism is a system whereby people who make money are rewarded by being able to reap the benefits of their labors. But even greater than that, because they have control of their money, capitalism also rewards those who create business and stimulate the economy.

It would be naïve to think there isn't greed and wickedness in capitalism. There is! But it is a system that affords us some of the greatest of all God-given human freedoms! Capitalism is the only system that has ever proven to create a strong economy and sustain that economy. The collapse of our banking system was not an accident. It was greedy people, fueled by decades of corrupt government that brought about a desired outcome... financial ruin for millions of Americans!

This corruption has been at work in our nation for decades.

You have to understand this corruption has been at work in our nation for decades. Socialism ruled most of the world during the time of President Franklin D. Roosevelt. It was the "happening thing." All the other nations had rulers. In Roosevelt's inaugural speech there were statements that suspiciously sounded as if he had hopes of ruling America in the fashion of the world scene. And just as socialism was creeping into America, it had already taken root in Europe.

The socialist movement in Europe created for itself a telling name. They called themselves Fabian Socialists. According to Wikipedia.org:

> The Fabian Society is a British socialist movement, whose purpose is to advance the principles of socialism via gradualist and reformist, rather than revolutionary, means. It is best known for its initial ground-breaking work beginning late in the 19th century and continuing up to World War I. The society laid many of the foundations of the Labour Party and subsequently affected the policies of states emerging from the decolonisation of the British Empire, especially India. The emblem of the society is the proverbial wolf in sheep's clothing.[4]

It is important to understand the key subtleties. Their goals were the same as those of all the socialists: a godless society that provided total domination of the masses by the elite. They would not, however, accomplish their goals by open war. They would do it by a gradual process of wearing down the enemy. This tactic was modeled by Quintus Fabius Maximus, a famous Roman general whose strategies advocated tactics of harassment and attrition rather than head-on battles. So rather than fight revolutions, the Fabian Socialists would wear people down by constant ongoing harassment. In such a battle as this there would be no standing up and declaring their positions and allowing people to decide if they were for them or against them. There would be slow methodical brainwashing and desensitization until what is obviously destructive is accepted as good, thereby creating the perfect cultural corruption!

As this movement came to the United States, they began to call themselves progressives. The progressives, like the Fabian Socialists in Europe, were godless people working a deceptive agenda through a war of attrition. However, the progressives developed a number of diabolic yet effective systematic processes whereby they would accomplish their goals. Because of the high value they have for their ideals, the end always justifies the means. Lying and deception are completely justified. Even the murder of innocent citizens is simply collateral damage. Socialist leaders around the world have murdered hundreds of millions of people in pursuit of their cause.

When Franklin Delano Roosevelt was elected president, the country was in a depression. It was not the great depression…just a depression. It became the great depression after Roosevelt took office and began to implement his plan called The New Deal. The New Deal that Roosevelt introduced was more than just a clever saying. It was actually a book written by a progressive that outlined how to accomplish the progressive agenda through government policies.

The New Deal didn't bring the country out of the Depression; in fact, according to some brilliant minds it made it worse. That's how it worsened to become the Great Depression. It actually took a world war to put enough people to work to pull America out of the Great Depression. It is in fact these same tactics that are being employed by our current government. Sustained financial crisis is the breeding ground for revolution and for facilitating the rise to power of dictators and false messiahs.

Reasonable people look at the economic situation in our country right now and, because they are reasonable they ask reasonable questions. In fact, everyone in America knows that if you spend more than you make you go bankrupt. If you keep spending and over-tax the people, you destroy the economy and private enterprise… then everyone goes bankrupt. You see, reasonable people are honest. They get up and go to work every day. They are not diabolical enough to imagine the lengths to which the world's elite will go to have absolute control of the planet. To paraphrase a great economist and historian, James Dale Davidson, the fall of every civilized nation is when

Everyone in America knows that if you spend more than you make you go bankrupt.

we begin to think that the whole world is civilized and will therefore respond to civilized reasoning.

It is common knowledge that more millionaires were made during the Great Depression than in any other time in the U.S. "During the years before 1929, as greater and greater amounts of credit was extended to individuals and businesses the economy was tipping over the edge from available cash to excessive amounts of credit debt. When the amount of extended credit reached a critical mass, and businesses failed to pay the credit bills, the companies crashed (the 1929 stock market crash). Because employees lost their jobs they could not pay their credit debts and the housing market and banking industries crashed."[5] In chaotic financial times coupled with the irrational fears stimulated by strategic nationwide propaganda, the wealth and the power will always change hands! What better way to ensure whose hands will gain control than to orchestrate the entire ordeal!

WHAT THE GOVERNMENT DOES

What we fail to understand is that governments are made up of people. If those people do not have righteousness in their heart, then they will give in to the uncontrollable lust for power. Remember the biblical word for righteousness means "as it should be."[6] There is a way that God intends for man to live: free, healthy, happy and independent. He wired us to thrive in love and peace. Governmental control beyond reasonable laws that protect people from one another and from government is a cancer to any society or any individual. Without constant vigilance those who make the laws will always succumb to the greed of making them for the benefit of their own agendas.

Through programs of entitlement—welfare, Social Security and Medicare—we have been lulled into a false sense of security by our government. But the cost of security, provided by someone else's hand, is always a loss of freedom. We have been told that the government will provide, so we have given away our power. Lord Acton said, "Power tends to corrupts, and absolute power corrupts absolutely." William Pitt, another British politician, said, "Unlimited power is apt to corrupt the minds of those who possess it." We corrupt our leaders by allowing them to make our choices! We allow politicians to stay in office too long. We do not hold them legally accountable to uphold the Constitution they were sworn to

We corrupt our leaders by allowing them to make our choices!

protect and uphold. We don't even hold them accountable for their campaign promises. We vote for them based on our party preference and then close our eyes while they dismantle our freedom and destroy our children!

You must remember that governments have no money and they make no money. When the government says, "We will take care of you," it is inviting you into a sleight-of-hand game where you make the money and they take it through taxes. Then they say to you, "In exchange for your loyalty we will give some of this back to you." To the poor they say, "If you will keep us in power, we will steal from those who know how to make money and give it to you." The unspoken message, however, is this: "We will not only keep you and future generations in poverty, but we will eventually have the entire nation in poverty. You have to be poor so we can have the money to fulfill our agenda and the cause is so great someone has to pay…you are that someone!"

The reasonable person, however, keeps asking reasonable questions. We think the battle is economics, but it's not. It's politics. We are seduced into thinking the debate is over health care, but health care is not the agenda; it's politics. We presume they are talking about education when they are actually fighting about indoctrination. We think abortion is a moral debate, it's not; it's population control and moral desensitization… political. Because of the lack of a moral compass of those in power, they will be more than glad to pretend we all are having the same discussion. As the rules of Quintus Fabius Maximus would dictate, the unspoken realities of the progressives are: "We will never tell you our true goals and no matter what agreements we make, we will break them. In fact, if you believe we have actually made agreements that will be honored, this buys us time to move ahead undetected. When you protest we will act as if we have been victimized. If you disagree with us, then we will attack you. We will slander you and destroy your reputation with any means possible. We will mask and hide our true agenda behind important issues like civil rights, religious freedom, freedom of speech and any other valiant cause. However, even when we speak the same words they will have different meanings. Like a drug addict navigating around his family's suspicions, we will keep you emotionally off balance with bogus issues; we will make you look guilty, we will play the victim, but we will never stop the deliberate pursuit of our drug of choice: control!" It is a debate that a reasonable person can never win. We will never hear the truth, and when it sounds like the truth it is little more than a political ruse.

To those who haven't lifted the veil and looked at the facts it might seem this is a battle between the Democrats and the Republicans. But it isn't. Eisenhower was a Republican, but he embraced many aspects of the New Deal. After Jimmy Carter passed horrible legislation that took us into a serious recession, established a cabinet level Department of Education and introduced banking laws that ultimately played into the economic debacle that threatens to ruin our country, there were *We are missing the bigger picture: the loss of freedom!* several Republicans and Democrats who could have changed those laws. Party affiliation is just another layer to the never ending cover-up. It is just another mask worn by those seeking to disguise the facts.

While Christians, minorities, those on the left and those on the right are voting and lobbying for their special interests, we have missed the big picture. While politicians are speaking "politic-ese" and seducing us through our special interests, we are missing the bigger picture: the loss of freedom! There is only one thing we can know about anyone: their track record. Until we look at how people voted, how they spent money

If the current political trends continue, we will face times never before seen in this country.

and how they upheld the Constitution we have no meaningful basis to make an intelligent voting decision.

GET READY TO TURN THE TIDE

By now you may be asking, "What does this have to do with prosperity and success?" If the current political trends continue, we will face economic collapse never before seen in this country. But there's more at stake. The strategy of Fabian Socialism reveals that their goal was to be achieved by "stealth, intrigue, subversion, and the deception of never calling socialism by its right name."[7] In other words, they will deceptively introduce fear and chaos into society in such a way that it becomes accepted as true and individuals will lose their belief in the opportunity of individual success. The end result of a loss of dreams, goals and vision, according to the wisdom of Proverbs, is destruction![8] When you lose the hope of creating a better future you will be destroyed by the powers that seek to control your life.

One of the top priorities of the socialist is to minimize human value. This is done first and foremost by destroying the reality that man is created in the likeness and image of God. This deception is the primary goal of the theory of evolution. Evolution is the golden key that holds the secret power to the progressive's degenerate agenda. If we are not created in the likeness and image of God we can introduce relativity, situational ethics and the removal of absolute morality. The taking of human life to accomplish a humanist agenda is not challenged in a godless society.

Soon after, there must be a complete lack of trust for the government. This has been done by the educational system that has portrayed our founders in the worst possible light. It is sustained by a biased news media that distorts the facts to fulfill its own agendas. Then there are the tactics of causing economic crashes, neutralizing our courts through political correctness and humanistic agendas. The very people who create the chaos are the politicians who are blaming the government and asking us to trust them. Then we somehow forget... they are the government.

Then the wealthy must be vilified as depriving the poor. Through education and a number of government-funded organizations and entitlement programs there is the full-blown propaganda that the wealthy are wicked and that if they had less, the poor would somehow have more. Amazingly those vilifying the rich are incredibly rich. Yet, they deflect attention from themselves by pointing at others. Then there is the final step...the creation of chaotic fear.

When I was a child, in grammar school, we actually practiced what we would do if America came under nuclear attack by the Soviets. I often wondered how a small wooden desk was going to protect me from a nuclear blast that was so powerful it was going to destroy human life as we knew it. But that's for another discussion. Then I remember hearing that we were going back into another ice age. At some point we were told we all would starve because of overpopulation. Now it's global warming. The government is systematically attempting to take over the food and water supply. It is essential that we be made to feel we are facing an obstacle so massive that there is no hope of survival unless the government saves us. When fear escalates through a manufactured cultural consciousness man will give away his freedom for the hope of a manufactured salvation. In that moment the wealth of the world will be in the hands of the wicked and the end of freedom has arrived.

In the philosophical world progressives seek to create those who succeed do so at the peril and loss of their fellow man. The humanistic propaganda that sounds so fair and reasonable will be the honey that disguises the taste of the bitter poison. The wealthy must give their money to the government so the government can redistribute the wealth according to its sense of fairness. In the name of making all people economically equal the elite will have to assume the humanitarian responsibility to explain reality to the masses while doling out the crumbs left over from a world once filled with endless wealth.

According to the greatest book of wisdom in the world, *"Upright citizens are good for a city and make it prosper, but the talk of the wicked tears it apart."* When enough people believe and speak from a heart of fear the world will be plunged into the fulfillment of the collective belief of its inhabitants and a new reality will be created. The only cure is found with those who believe in a world created by a loving God who gave us enough

It will be those who believe in success and free enterprise who will turn the trend from a world of disaster to a world of opportunity.

provision to last as long as man is here. It will be those who believe in success and free enterprise who will turn the trend from a world of disaster to a world of opportunity.

In Heart Physics® we don't just teach people how to make money. There are many wonderful schools, seminars and books that can teach you how to make money. We help you establish a heart for success and prosperity! Without success in your heart, opportunity is lost no matter what the economy or the political environment! Until success is in your heart opportunity is defined by your circumstances. When success is in your heart, your beliefs create opportunity!

CHAPTER 23

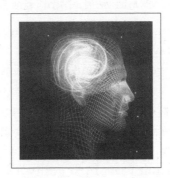

CHANGING THE WORLD
THROUGH SUCCESS

When the government offers equality,
it means we will all be equally poor!

A s a child I was subtly tilted toward socialism. No, I didn't grow up in another country, nor were my parents anti-American. They were as American as apple pie. But then, you may have been influenced in your formative years just as I was.

We were very poor. My mother supported us on a meager salary she earned as a clerk in a small clothing store. In the cold winters in Tennessee my brother and I would either shovel coal or cut wood to heat the tiny wood frame house from the single cast-iron stove in the center of the room.

Many of our meals were desperately deficient of nutrients. In lean times there were a lot of flapjacks, basically flour and water with a little milk gravy to give it some taste. When my grandmother would buy us a few extra groceries we would have a few days of eating well. Most of the time, however, it was meager yet adequate. Many nights we sat down to things we really didn't like, but that was all we had. More than once, in response to our protests, our mother would reply with, "Children in China are starving tonight. You should be thankful you have food."

Although it was never said, I can remember forming the distinct impression that by me having food it somehow took food away from children somewhere in the world. Growing up in a conservative society with puritanical roots further enforced this corrupt logic. In my formative years there was some philosophical root that made me believe, at a very subtle level, that for anyone to have, it took something away from someone else. The result was a deep sense of guilt associated with material possessions. For many of my young adult years I felt guilty if I had more than one pair of shoes or too many clothes. I felt I was involved in some injustice to the needy.

PEOPLE SUFFER WITHOUT CAPITALISM

This is the philosophy that has infiltrated our schools and universities. From grade school to post graduate school the ideologies of socialism have permeated the younger generation, closing their eyes to the biblical mandate for free enterprise. Our country has lost its moral middle ground. People either struggle with guilt for having or they are driven by an insatiable greed that is never satisfied. The Bible provides a mandate for free enterprise but warns of the corruption of greed! In fact, the Bible presents the idea that both lack and abundance have their own inherent temptations.[1]

The truth is no one in the world suffers because of what I have. In fact, just the opposite is true. Every time I purchase a pair of pants I employ hundreds of people. The farmer who grew the cotton; the companies that developed the seed, the farm equipment, the fertilizer and pesticides; the worker who harvested it; the cotton gin workers; the mill workers who made it into fabric; the engineers who develop that equipment; the workers who maintain it, the people who made the thread; the sowers who sowed the fabric together; the people who made the buttons and the zippers; the truck drivers who moved each of those products from place to place through each different stage of production. But it doesn't stop there. There was the fashion designer; the photographer who put it in a magazine; the ad agency who brokered the deal between the distributor and the ad firm; the people who harvested the tress that made the paper for the magazine; the people who made the ink; the computer operator who laid out the ad; the writer who wrote the sales copy; the printer who printed the magazine; the post office who carried the magazine to my house; the fuel that goes into my car to drive to the store and all the people involved in that entire process; the salesperson who waited on me in the store; the janitor who cleans the store; the security guard who guards the store. Then there is the armored car company that picks up the money and takes it to the bank and then we get into the bank employees. That doesn't include the administrative staff, the bookkeepers and accountant and finally all the government employees who are involved in all the different aspects of the business and taxes. When I cannot afford to buy things, the entire world suffers because children in China will go hungry when I do not spend money. Today their families are making many of these products.

Then there is the idea that the rich are somehow responsible to provide for the poor. Ethically the rich should be compassionate on those who have needs. But when the government takes money from one person to give to another it is theft. Generosity is what you do with your own money, not what you do with someone else's money. Taking from the rich and giving to the poor sounds noble, in a Robin Hood sort of fantasy, but it is theft, not generosity. I fully support programs that provide for the disabled, the elderly and those who cannot take care of themselves. But entitlement programs that give to the irresponsible with no accountability are not only foolish they are destructive to every element of society. When offered with no accountability they encourage laziness, codependency, entitlement and victim mentalities. The growth of the poverty in

When the government takes money from one person to give to another it is theft.

our country has grown through these demeaning programs that offer a handout with no hope of self-development.

If I allow an entrepreneur to keep his earnings, he will do what he has always done. He will find ways to put his money to work. He will create commerce, which creates jobs. Yes, he will get richer, but that is the reward for hard work and diligence. However, history shows us that when we give money to irresponsible people they simply continue to do irresponsible things. They buy more cigarettes, alcohol and drugs. This is why the Bible solemnly warns against giving to people who will not work.[2]

SOCIALISM DEVALUES THE POOR

Does this mean I am prejudiced against the poor? Absolutely not! In fact it is just the opposite; I am compassionate. I was poor. I come from a long family line of substance abuse, codependency and poverty! What a poor person needs is an education and an opportunity… not a handout! It is the lack of responsibility and accountability in our social programs that continue to send the message to the poor, "You are incapable, and you will amount to nothing."

Mine is not an isolated story; millions of people have risen from poverty to be wealthy, successful, influential members of society. But for every success story there are millions of people who have succumbed to a system that is built on codependency and control, who have lost their sense of dignity and worth. There are now third and possibly fourth generation welfare recipients who have been given a heritage of self-doubt, low self-worth, irresponsibility and codependency. When we reward bad behavior and low productivity it becomes the way of the society!

The socialist, progressive agenda is to create a codependent nation that has no God to trust so they look to the government to provide. In the absence of the dignity that comes from knowing we are created in the likeness and image of God we devolve to a lower existence that does not inspire greatness. We become human drones with no motivation to achieve.

While America and capitalism are being vilified around the world you might take notice of this: When a natural disaster occurs anywhere in the world we are the first to arrive with aid. The same countries who malign us for our prosperity are the first to criticize us if we don't rescue other nations. It is rare that you ever see a purely socialistic country help another country of the world.

> *In socialism, we become human drones with no motivation to achieve.*

The "fall of communism" in the former Soviet Union resulted from the dire poverty it created. Socialism has never in all of human history succeeded. But those citizens don't know it because what they hear and think is controlled by the government. Only during the Great Depression have Americans stood in bread lines. Only during the Carter administration have we had gas rationing in recent history. Why? During every financial collapse in America there has been an attempt to derail free enterprise, create chaos and install socialism. We have broken free from those economic downward spirals when we returned to the free enterprise, capitalist philosophies...with all its flaws.

You never hear of missionaries being sent out from a socialist country. In most of those countries true believers in any religion would be imprisoned or controlled. But even if they could go, where would the money come from? The greatest inventions, the inspiring innovations and the great breakthroughs most consistently come from free people in a system that inspires and rewards productivity and success.

Not only has socialism never worked, but the government interfering in private enterprise has never worked.

In Russia prior to the year 2000, 4 percent of the tillable land was owned by the people while 96 percent of the tillable land was owned by government. Thirty percent of all the beef in Russia came from the 4 percent of privately owned land. Over half of the dairy products also came from the privately owned land. Not only has socialism never worked, but the government interfering in private enterprise has never worked. America has proven that over and over again. Our postal service is in collapse. Social security is broke—not only broke, but realize the government violated dozens of ethical principles and federal laws that govern the average business. They collected money earmarked for our retirement and spent it on other projects with no accountability. Medicare is broke and filled with corruption. Likewise, Fannie Mae and Freddie Mac led the housing crash through theft and mismanagement. We could write an entire book on programs the government gets involved in, drives into the ground and, after they have stolen all the money and mismanaged these programs, steal even more of our money through taxes to cover their injustice. Today in Canada their health care consumes 50 percent of their budget. It is estimated that within five years it will take 100 percent of the budget. Socialism doesn't work, has never worked and will never work! The moment we trust others to manage our money all sanity is lost!

History is full of lessons about the power of free enterprise. After World War II, India and Japan both began to develop their capabilities to make steel. Japan put the ownership of the steel mills in the hands of the people; India put theirs in the hands of the government. Less than 50 years later Japan was producing 100 times more steel than India. But what makes this most interesting is that, of the two main ingredients for making steel—coal and iron ore—Japan had neither while India was rich with both. People always prosper when the opportunity for reward is based on their ability for personal prosperity.

GOVERNMENT'S BIG SECRET

There is a closely held secret the government does not want you to know. True capitalists, entrepreneurs and industrialists know this secret. The only people who do not know it are the poor, the ignorant and the seduced. Here is the secret: The government can't create one job. It cannot improve our economy; it can only interfere with it. *The government doesn't make any money, people do.* The government doesn't have any money, people do. Even if someone goes to work for the government, he or she is being paid by you. Therefore, creating a government job does not help the economy. It hurts the economy because you will be taxed to pay for that job. The only people who create jobs and improve the quality of our nation are people who understand and use success in a healthy manner. Take the money away from the capitalists and give it to the government, the worst known managers of money in the world, and we will all be broke!

Then there is another big lie the government does not want you to know. They claim they will use the dollars they take from the wealthy to make people equal—you know, equal opportunity, no child left behind and various entitlement programs. Since every way the government approaches these agendas demotivates man it cannot make a poor man equal to a rich man. It cannot make people of different races have equal opportunity. And since kids can't actually fail in school or be disciplined, they have no motivation to learn. These are things that happen in the heart of a man, not in his circumstance. People find equality when they have equal opportunity and equal reward…and equal opportunity for failure.

The only way the government can make people equal is by making people equally poor. If we take enough money away from the wealthy, we all will be poor. The only way the corrupt system can give an equal education and ensure everyone will pass is to lower the standard of the education. By reducing everyone to the lowest common denominator the government claims to make us all equal. The only way the government can give us equal opportunity is by making sure none of us have any real opportunity.

> *The only way the government can make people equal is by making people equally poor.*

Entitlement is part of the propaganda of equality and compassion. Entitlement programs are not driven by a deep compassion to help people. Entitlement programs are a means to buying votes from people who have been convinced that they have no fair opportunity. It is driven by a humanistic idealism that opposes America, God and human dignity on every level. It takes away one of the most God-like characteristics of man. We are the only species who can improve the quality of life by our own personal choices. This is the heritage of a people made in the likeness and image of God! By making people dependent on the government they never discover their true ability to create and prosper. Entitlement engenders gross codependency…people doing for others what they could and should do for themselves. If they don't have the means to do for themselves, then teach them to earn, teach them to compete, build their self confidence through self discipline—but make them responsible by having an equal opportunity to succeed or fail!

If our nation is to become great again and remain great, it will happen through people who believe in the positive power of personal success. We must give up many of our personal interests and put politicians in power who believe in our Constitution and free enterprise. We must look past the complete farce of the two party system and create a government that works regardless of the party they serve. In fact, if they serve the party, they are disqualified to serve the people. We must resist every form of government that seeks to invade the private sector. We must recover our schools and put an end to the reign of socialist, anti-God propaganda.

It is time for us to enter into that great paradox of having a healthy desire for wealth but living free of greed and self-indulgence. If we use our wealth for those things that truly contribute to life, then we will once again inspire the entire world. We will be a light on the hill. We will give jobs to billions of people around the world. But most of all we will preserve our most basic human freedoms.

This paradox can only be found when it is first established in the heart. Heart Physics® creates a basis for success that will not destroy the successful. A heart that is established in true wealth finds contentment so that money can be used for its intended purpose! Holistic wealth is a product of the heart. Holistic wealth brings health and prosperity to us and the world we live in! When people who have a heart for a holistic success have the money they will to help the world.

CHAPTER 24

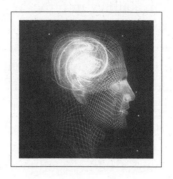

JOURNEY TO THE CENTER
OF YOUR WORLD

God will take you where your mind has not been willing to go.

I F YOU ARE LIKE the majority of people I meet, you either have little awareness of your heart or have learned to ignore its subtle voice. The soft intuitive voice of the heart can be hard to hear amidst the panicking, frenzied demands of the mind. But even if you're a seasoned internal observer you can still learn by reviewing some of these basic heart realities.

This journey into your heart is a journey into the center, the seat, the source of your very being. It puts you in touch with the real you, and for the first time in your life gives you the power over the real you. Your life stops running on the destructive autopilot of negative beliefs etched on your heart by life's traumas. For the first time you have the unique opportunity available only to one species—human beings created in the likeness and image of God—the ability to change the quality of your life by changing your beliefs.

BEGINNING THE JOURNEY

Some people fear this journey into the heart. Life's failures, moral flaws and self-criticism have become such a mental way of life that we fear the heart will only produce a magnification of the mind's endless negativity. But when we escape the negative control of the mind we enter a world where there just "is." There is not the nagging judgment and criticism of the mind. We no longer hear the voices of our critical parents. We are beyond the touch of those who have abused us. We are the only ones in our heart. In the heart we observe, we learn and we grow, free from all the negativity! We observe what "is" without judgment!

Those who are deeply conflicted have spent their life controlling their thoughts by activity, noise (radio and television), over-socialization, drugs, alcohol or mental and physical disorders created to avoid facing self. Yes, the pain we experience from our internal hurts is so strong that the heart often creates disease because it is easier to cope with physical pain than the pain of a broken heart. When these people first experience relaxation they feel as if they are losing control. They fear that the loss of control will constitute an overflow of the very emotions they are holding at bay.

If we look in our heart long enough we will always come upon a picture of the perfect us living in perfect love and peace with a loving God!

When we get into our Heart Zone the only things that can occur are the things we allow. If we tell ourselves we will only see what we are ready to face, that's what our heart will allow. In every Heart Physics® module we always add aspects of the process that create great peace and comfort. But because God speaks in our heart, we can be assured He will never show us a negative picture of ourselves. God draws us to a better future with hope, not guilt. Guilt is the programmed response of our conscience to that which conflicts with the way we were originally wired. If we look in our heart long enough we will always come upon a picture of the perfect us living in perfect love and peace with a loving God!

PARADOXES OF THE HEART

When moving in the heart one is faced with an endless barrage of paradoxes. External factors are like Newtonian physics—they are pretty simple. They are perceived, understood and explained in a linear fashion. Something is or isn't. It is good or it is bad. But as we move inward to work from the heart everything becomes a paradox. Linear concepts no longer apply; we are now viewing our life through the continuum. This is not the deceptive substitute of relativism. This is getting beyond the legalism of rules and considering all the aspect of the heart. Like the physicist who first observes and reaches a conclusion through the laws of Newtonian physics, when he looks deeper, suddenly an entirely new set of laws applies: quantum physics. His definitions determined by Newtonian physics were correct if he was seeking only to define that which is manifested externally. But to look deeper, those laws no longer apply. Now a completely different understanding emerges because the event is perceived from a new vantage point...the internal.

When viewing my actions through the continuum they are no longer simply good or bad. They often have degrees of both. This means I can no longer mask my motives in the legalism of rules. As I learn to live from my heart I observe and own all that is present in every behavior. Only with this completely honest internal inventory can I ever break myself from the destructive patterns of past failures and actually turn those failures into learning experiences.

PARADOX: NO BLAME

The freedom to look inside and perform an honest inventory can happen only when we enter into a new paradox: total acceptance of responsibility and absolutely no blame. Blame blinds the mind to what the heart really sees. Many people are afraid to take a personal heart inventory because they are afraid of what they will see. People who are afraid of what they will see will never take responsibility for their actions and they will never be free. They will never really know the deep motives, fears or negative emotions that drive some of what seems to be admirable behavior.

One of the first laws of transformation is, "I can change only that over which I have control. I have control only of that which is mine. I have owned only that for which I am placing no blame." I can't blame me, I can't blame others, I can't blame God…I can't blame anyone if I want to get out of my problem.

Blame focuses on who will be punished; responsibility focuses on who will respond with healing action. If I assume responsibility, then I am acknowledging, "No matter who did what to get me into this, I am able to respond and get me out of this! I have control over me and my responses!" The most liberating freedom in the world is personal responsibility. In fact, personal freedom never actually exceeds personal responsibility!

> *The most liberating freedom in the world is personal responsibility.*

Regardless of our religious or anti-religious beliefs, we are wired the same way. We have no capacity for guilt. The religious and non-religious have an internal moving away from guilt, which usually means some form of self-deception. Blaming others is the most convenient. The religious fear that being wrong will cause God to reject them, so they must blame someone. But the truly spiritually minded person knows and trusts the unconditional love of a merciful God and Creator. We have no need to hide, cover or otherwise avoid responsibility. So the first law of internal awareness is a willingness to see anything about ourselves with no guilt or blame.

The first governing law of transformation facilitates the second: vigilance. The wisest man to live warned us to be ever vigilant in guarding our heart. Guarding is something that occurs because someone is paying attention. We should set a guard at the door of our heart and always notice what is really driving us internally! It is only this ever-present awareness that will protect us from repeated failure and self-deception.

As we have previously learned, peace is the primary state that facilitates heart awareness and direction. When at peace we notice the slightest disturbance. When in chaos we can be overtaken by that which is obvious to all but ourselves. When determining our value for peace, we must remember that in one moment of emotional turmoil we can make decisions that can take a lifetime to overcome. Or worse, it could cost us our life. Likewise, in one moment we may recognize the opportunity that will forever change our financial world.

Everyone I know who makes this journey makes noticing a way of life. At first it's hard to notice our actual driving factors in the heat of the moment. In those situations we have to look back to understand. We get in our Heart Zone and review past actions. In Heart Physics® we teach people how to look, from a heart perspective, on past decisions and actions to understand what was really driving the behavior, with no guilt. From that internal view, new decisions can be made about how those things will be handled. In the absence of guilt taking ownership is easy. Then the door is opened to write a new, empowering belief on the heart.

PARADOX: THE CEILING OF BELIEFS

Another paradox of the heart is that you can never rise above the beliefs of the heart. At first glance one would ask, "What's the use? I'm stuck! What's the point in trying?" God is always speaking inspiration in your heart. He is always attempting to bring you into an incredible quality of life beyond your current experience. When that inspiration comes it can be the doorway to an entirely new world, yet it will be an unknown path.

Inspiration is an invitation to step into a new dimension of life. But we know our life, as a whole, cannot exceed our sense of self. A call to a new quality of life usually means a call to a new quality of character. That doesn't always mean our present character is bad; it just means to go where we are going next we will have to change. "But, I thought the mind resisted change?" It does, unless we can find a way to feel peace and confidence in the process of change.

Facing change confidently comes from two primary sources. One is to use the tools for heart work to preview the change. See the end before it occurs and it becomes familiar. Enjoy the end before it occurs and it becomes desirable. Believe the end before it occurs and it becomes unchangeable! Heart tools give us the capacity to cross any bridge and climb any mountain.

The ultimate secret for facing growth and change is trust for the One inspiring the change.

The ultimate secret for facing growth and change is trust for the One inspiring the change. The psalmist said when he walked through the valley of the shadow of death he would not be afraid.[1] Even though he was in threatening territory, his confidence came from the Shepherd, the One who was leading him! The absolute belief that God is good and only good; that He has never hurt you and He will not hurt you; that everything He does is an expression of deep personal love; these are the beliefs that make the valley of the shadow of death powerless to hinder your journey.

So the great paradox is this: My heart will not allow me to go into the unknown so how will I ever follow God into greater wealth, success, health and happiness? Herein is one of the greatest of all secrets of transformation. If God is my "known" and I trust Him completely, then it matters little what potential dangers lay ahead on the path. If He is my peace, the path cannot be my fear.

I have heard stories about those brave souls who, during the Vietnam War, navigated through treacherous battlefield entrapments. When traversing enemy minefields there was one rule: Walk in the steps of the person leading the way. This means you were not looking for the mines. Your focus was not on the potential explosives. Your focus was on the footprints of the person leading the way. God wants you to enjoy success in every dimension of your life. If you focus on the pitfalls of the unknown path, then every step is treacherous. But if you simply follow in His step as He breathes wisdom into your heart, then you will hardly notice the fearful possibilities of the unknown!

As much as this sounds like a cliché, I have to say it: It's not the destination; it's the journey. There is no destination when dealing with the heart. Every day the world around us is changing. Every day our needs are changing. Nothing is staying the same except God. He is always good. What worked in last year's economy may not work today. Every aspect of life contains so many variables that it is impossible for the conscious mind to know all it needs to know. But the heart… the place where God speaks, where we have access to unlimited wisdom and limitless possibility, this is where we will find the map to make the journey.

The Bible tells us that God gives us the power, the capacity and the strength to get wealth.[2] True success and prosperity is always a journey into the heart to hear the inspiration of a loving God!

CHAPTER 25

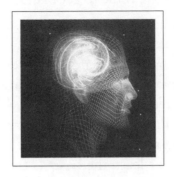

A COMPREHENSIVE APPROACH

The more of your senses you influence at one time,
the quicker and easier the transformation.

While there is so much more to learn about the heart, you know enough to make the most incredible changes in your life. Read and reread every page of this book until you can put every aspect of it into practice. Transformation doesn't come by what you know; it comes by what you believe and put into practice. Finally you can break past the world of behavior modification and external motivation and change what is actually driving you internally. Then you can experience behavior modification and external motivation in a way that brings peace, joy and positive results instead of frustration and self-judgment!

> *Transformation doesn't come by what you know; it comes by what you believe and put into practice.*

SUCCESS IS YOUR DESTINY

Heart Physics® is not a gimmick. It is a tool. It is not a religion. Yet it utilizes tools that are common to most major religions and cultures.

Heart Physics® was developed from biblical practices and principles, yet you don't have to believe the Bible to get major aspects of it to work.

Heart Physics® is based on a few simple principles. The principles are not only biblically based but also scientifically verified. God created everything based on a consistent logic and wisdom. At the deepest level there are no contradictions in all that exists. That which can be seen, or in other words, all that is created—the physical world—is a reflection of that which cannot be seen.[1] The world and all that exists is in an interactive relationship with mankind and is becoming what we believe it will become. Last but not by any means least, the heart is the seat of man, the seat of believing and the seat of the power that works in man. As we are in our hearts, so are we in life![2]

My understanding of our Creator is that more than anything else He is love. All that He does is an expression of His value for mankind, the degree of preciousness He has for us, and the high degree in which He holds us. Religion may have managed to make us believe otherwise, but the Bible and all of creation reveals something different.

Success and prosperity with purpose is our God-given destiny and heritage.

We were originally wired to live in paradise. Our programming has led us to accept and expect much less than we could and should have. The world, despite the messages of those who seek to control us through fear, will produce enough resources to sustain man indefinitely. Success and prosperity with purpose is our God-given destiny and heritage.

By influencing our heart we have the capacity to reprogram ourselves and return to a version of life much more in line with the original intention. By listening to our heart we can hear the infinite wisdom of a loving God that will always lead us into the very best life has to offer.

The two main enemies of transformation are self-accusation and time. The quicker we bring about change the greater the likelihood that we will. "If you snooze, you lose," may have never been truer in any setting. The greater the gap between inspiration and application the more the likelihood of deflation! So the best strategy is, without overwhelming yourself, put as many things into application as possible, starting now!

In order to make this as easy as possible, always remember you are not doing these exercises to create wealth. You are doing these exercises to change your heart. As your heart changes, you will find yourself thinking differently. You will recognize opportunities that you have never before noticed. You will meet and respond to people differently. You will start making the connections that had previously eluded you. You will have a greater confidence to act on your inspirations. You may find, as many have, that you have more physical energy to pursue your dreams and goals. You are not trying to force prosperity and success. However, by influencing your heart you facilitate prosperity and success.

While you have learned more than enough to make this work just by reading this book, you may find yourself desiring more personal involvement with someone making the journey and sense the value of a coach. Through our Creating Wealth Program we reinforce the tools you've learned, introduce you to new tools and show you how to put them into practice. We provide you with an arsenal of approaches so you can design your multi-modality approach to bring the greatest influence in the shortest amount of time. Plus you get hours of personal contact and daily encouragement from me. Through our program I give you the same coaching, through recordings that you would get if we were to meet every day. In some ways the recorded program is better because there are no time restraints. You can back up and listen to it over and over again until you milk every sentence of every ounce of life-transforming power!

The following will serve as a reminder of the tools you have learned and a glimpse into some of the tools you can discover.

MULTI-MODALITY APPROACH

Ancient Principles (Life Management): The time-honored rules of life management for creating wealth.

Develop Life Skills: Learn everything you can about the area you choose to explore for your financial growth.

Limiting Beliefs Meditation: The most incredible tool for identifying and uninstalling destructive beliefs and installing new empowering beliefs.

Wise Counsel: Find someone who has succeeded in the field of your choice and allow him or her to mentor you.

Creating Wealth Subliminal Support: Use this powerful tool to keep you encouraged and on track as you implement your plan.

Painting a New Life Picture: This simple seven-minute exercise will catapult you into a new dimension of transforming your beliefs.

Daily Heart Work: Be sure to use any of the many tools available to daily establish your heart in the life beliefs that support your goals.

Tools for Transformation

- The Prayer Organizer
- Pain and Pleasure Exercise
- Releasing
- Heart Physics®
- Prayer
- Mini-meditations
- Confession/Affirmation
- Put Off, Put On
- Interrupt the destructive pattern
- The rubber band
- Put on a new belief of choice
- Casting down vain imaginations
- Overcoming negative and destructive thoughts and imaginations that create negative, destructive emotions

For more information about Heart Physics® and all the modules we offer, visit www.heartyphysics.com. Go to DrJamesBRichards.com and sign up for my blog or daily tweet and facebook messages designed to keep you encouraged and making progress.

So this is it…. This is your chance to change all your negative programming and move the financial boundaries in your life. Now you can get everything you've ever learned about success to actually work! As you transform your personal beliefs and create a life picture of the true you, the more you will experience positive, painless, effortless transformation into a life better than anything you've ever imagined!

Remember, with God all things are possible. Now that you will be listening to the one place God speaks—your heart—you will discover the limitless possibility of success without boundaries!

ENDNOTES

Chapter 1

1. Drs. Alex Loyd and Ben Johnson, *The Healing Code* (Peoria, Arizona: Intermedia Publishing Group, Inc., 2010), 100.
2. Deuteronomy 8:18.

Chapter 3

1. 1 Timothy 6:10a NLT.
2. See Titus 1:15.
3. Proverbs 1:32b KJV.

Chapter 4

1. Pat Shannan, "Scientists Confirm U.S. Has World's Biggest Oil Reserves" AmericanFreePress.nct, Issue #26, July 29, 2009. http://www.americanfreepress.net/html/biggest_oil_reserves_182.html.
2. Facts about coal, clean-energy.us. Accessed October 12, 2010. http://www.clean-energy.us/facts/coal.htm.

Chapter 5

1. Dr. John G. Kappas, *Professional Hypnotism Manual* (Tarzana, California: Panorama Publishing Company, 2001), 8.
2. See Matthew 7:1-2. Read James B. Richards, *How to Stop the Pain* (New Kensington, Pennsylvania: Whitaker House, 2001).
3. Mark 9:23b.

Chapter 6

1. Tony Robbins, *Personal Power* (San Diego, California: Robbins Research Internationl, Inc., 1993).
2. Mark 7:13a NIV.

3. *Thayer's Greek Lexicon*, PC Study Bible formatted Electronic Database. Copyright © 2000, 2003, 2006 by Biblesoft, Inc.
4. *Biblesoft's New Exhaustive Strong's Numbers and Concordance with Expanded Greek-Hebrew Dictionary*. Copyright © 1994, 2003, 2006 Biblesoft, Inc. and International Bible Translators, Inc.

Chapter 7

1. The Greek word for righteousness literally means "as it should be." (*Thayer's Greek Lexicon*, PC Study Bible formatted Electronic Database. Copyright © 2000, 2003, 2006 by Biblesoft, Inc.) A righteous heart is a heart that believes in life as it should be, according to God's promises.
2. Drs. Alex Loyd and Ben Johnson, *The Healing Code* (Peoria, Arizona: Intermedia Publishing Group, Inc., 2010), 102.
3. Ibid., 103.

Chapter 8

1. King Solomon, Ecclesiastes 9:11.
2. Proverbs 10:22.
3. James Strong, *Strong's Exhaustive Concordance of the Bible* (Nashville, Tennessee: Holman Bible Publishers, n.d.), #H6089.

Chapter 9

1. "Heart Zone" is a terminology used in Heart Physics® that describes the state of meditation one enters when he or she is able to influence his or her heart.

Chapter 10

1. Doc Childre and Deborah Rozman, *Transforming Stress* (Oakland, California: New Harbinger Publications, Inc., 2005), x.

Chapter 11

1. See Proverbs 23:7.
2. Laird Harris, Gleason L. Archer, Jr., Bruce K. Waltke, *Theological Wordbook of the Old Testament*, Vol. II (Chicago, Illinois: The Moody Bible Institute of Chicago, 1981), 557.
3. Mark 4:24 AMP: *"And He said to them, Be careful what you are hearing. The measure [of thought and study] you give [to the truth you hear] will be the measure [of virtue and knowledge] that comes back to you—and more [besides] will be given to you who hear."*

Chapter 12

1. Doc Childre and Howard Martin, *The HeartMath Solution* (New York: Harper Collins Publishing, 1999), 4.

Chapter 13

1. See Proverbs 4:23.

Chapter 14

1. Stephen Covey, *The 7 Habits of Highly Effective People* (New York: Simon & Schuster, 1989), 18.
2. From lectures of the Hypnosis Motivation Institute, Tarzana, California.
3. Drs. Alex Loyd and Ben Johnson, *The Healing Code* (Peoria, Arizona: Intermedia Publishing Group, Inc., 2010), 177.
4. Proverbs 1:32 KJV.

Chapter 16

1. See James 2:26.

Chapter 17

1. You can read Jesus' parable of the wheat and tares in Matthew 13:24-30.

Chapter 18

1. Matthew 7:7 KJV.
2. Kenneth S. Wuest, *Studies in the Vocabulary of the Greek New Testament*, Volume III of *Word Studies in the Greek New Testament* (Grand Rapids, Michigan: Wm. B. Eerdmans Publishing Company, 1973), 96.
3. You can read this parable in Luke 8:5-18.
4. See Mark 4:24 AMP.

Chapter 19

1. James Strong, *Strong's Exhaustive Concordance* (Grand Rapids, Michigan: Baker Book House, 1984).
2. *Thayer's Greek Lexicon*, PC Study Bible formatted Electronic Database. Copyright © 2000, 2003, 2006 by Biblesoft, Inc.

Chapter 20

1. See Hebrews 4:11 KJV.

Chapter 21

1. Drs. Alex Loyd and Ben Johnson, *The Healing Code* (Peoria, Arizona: Intermedia Publishing Group, Inc., 2010), 49.
2. Romans 3:17.
3. Colossians 3:15a.
4. *Thayer's Greek Lexicon*, PC Study Bible formatted Electronic Database. Copyright © 2000, 2003, 2006 by Biblesoft, Inc. and *Biblesoft's New Exhaustive Strong's Numbers and Concordance with Expanded Greek-Hebrew Dictionary*. Copyright © 1994, 2003, 2006 Biblesoft, Inc. and International Bible Translators, Inc.

Chapter 22

1. Ephesians 2:2.
2. Christine Lagorio, "U.S. Education Slips In Rankings," Sept. 13, 2005, cbsnews.com.
3. Ibid.
4. Fabian Society, wikipedia.org, (accessed 10/14/10).
5. Sandra Simmons, "Secret To Becoming A Millionaire During A Depression," www.buzzle.com. Accessed November 4, 2010. http://www.buzzle.com/articles/secret-to-becoming-a-millionaire-during-a-depression.html.
6. *Thayer's Greek Lexicon*, PC Study Bible formatted Electronic Database. Copyright © 2000, 2003, 2006 by Biblesoft, Inc.
7. Source unknown.
8. See Proverbs 29:18.
9. Proverbs 11:11 NLT.

Chapter 23

1. See Proverbs 30:8-9.
2. See 2 Thessalonians 3:10.

Chapter 24

1. See Psalm 23:4.
2. See Deuteronomy 8:18.

Chapter 25

1. See Romans 1:20.
2. See Proverbs 23:7.

PERSONAL SUCCESS INVENTORY

Make these statements and use the method of testing that is most comfortable for you.

Add you own list of statements to expand your Personal Success Inventory.

- I want to experience greater prosperity.
- I am ready to experience financial abundance.
- I am confident in my ability to prosper.
- Greater prosperity will make my life better.
- I believe success should be hard.

Now we will test for:

- God wants me to prosper.
- I have the capacity to experience greater success.
- I have released all fear related to prosperity.
- I have released all guilt that would limit my prosperity.

ABOUT THE AUTHOR

JAMES RICHARDS IS A PIONEER in the field of faith-based human development. He has combined spirituality, energy medicine, scientific concepts and human intuition into a philosophical approach that brings about congruence in spirit, soul and body, resulting in incredible breakthroughs in health, emotional management and financial abundance. He is a life coach, consultant, teacher and motivational trainer. He holds doctorates in Theology, Oriental Medicine and Human Behavior. He was awarded an honorary doctorate for years of service in the Philippines. His many certifications include: substance abuse counselor, detox specialist, herbalist, handwriting analysis, EFT, energy medicine and an impressive number of additional certifications and training certificates.

Dr. Richards has been successful as an entrepreneur who has built several successful businesses ranging from contracting to real estate to marketing. As a national best-selling author, Dr. Richards has written several books that have sold several million copies around the world. His most noted work is Heart Physics®, a life renewal program designed to equip people to transform any aspect of their life through changing the beliefs of their heart.

When asked why he has studied such a broad field his answer is simple: "If it helps people, I want to understand it!" The goal of all his work is to "help people experience wholeness: spirit, soul and body!"

OTHER BOOKS BY DR. JAMES B. RICHARDS:

How to Stop the Pain

Becoming the Person You Want to Be

Breaking the Cycle

Grace: The Power to Change

The Gospel of Peace

Escape from Codependent Christianity

How to Write, Publish and Market Your Own Bestseller

Satan Unmasked

We Still Kiss

Supernatural Ministry

The Prayer Organizer

Effective Small Group Ministry in the New Millennium

My Church, My Family: How to Have a Healthy Relationship with the Church

Taking the Limits Off God

Leadership that Builds People, Volume I: Developing the Heart of a Leader

Leadership that Builds People, Volume II: Developing Leaders Around You

The Anatomy of a Miracle

To contact Dr. Richards, call or write:
Impact Ministries
3516 S. Broad Place
Huntsville, AL 35805
256-536-9402
256-536-4530 - Fax
www.impactministries.com

Positive, Painless, Permanent, Effortless Transformation

essential heart physics

DR. JAMES B. RICHARDS
research

In just 30 days you can discover the ultimate secret to a limitless life! In this life-changing program you will discover the keys to removing your personal boundaries.

Our limitations are nothing more than the boundaries created by faulty beliefs. All we need is the key to open the door that moves us past this lifetime of destructive thinking. All through history the key has represented knowledge, the power of entrance, and unlimited access. In the Essential Heart Physics® Program you will receive the *Heart-Key* that, in essence, will give you unlimited access to your heart, bypassing years of faulty logic and reason.

You can simply open the door of your heart and experience:

· A connection to the miraculous.
· Unshakable faith.
· A healthy, positive sense of self-worth!
· The power to change your beliefs at will!
· The unconditional love and acceptance of God!
· Christ, the Great Healer, in you!
· A new confidence!

And...conquer stress, anger, and negative emotions!

Essential Heart Physics® will open the eyes of your heart to see the "unseen" and introduce you to the realm of positive, painless, permanent, effortless transformation.

Order this life-changing program TODAY!
Impact Ministries
256.536.9402 • www.impactministries.com